SCOTT FORESMAN

Art

Robyn Montana Turner, Ph.D.
Program Author

PEARSON

Scott
Foresman

Editorial Offices: Glenview, Illinois • Parsippany, New Jersey • New York, New York

Sales Offices: Needham, Massachusetts • Duluth, Georgia • Glenview, Illinois • Coppell, Texas • Sacramento, California • Mesa, Arizona

Program Consultants

Christopher Adejumo, Ph.D.
Associate Professor
  Visual Art Studies
  University of Texas
  Austin, Texas

Doug Blandy, Ph.D.
Professor and Director
  Arts and Administration Program
  Institute for Community Arts and Studies
  University of Oregon
  Eugene, Oregon

Rebecca Brooks, Ph.D.
Professor
  Department of Art and Art History
  University of Texas
  Austin, Texas

Sara A. Chapman, M.Ed.
Director of Fine Arts
  Alief Independent School District
  Houston, Texas

James M. Clarke, M.Ed.
Executive Director
  Texas Coalition for Quality Arts Education
  Houston, Texas

Georgia Collins, Ph.D.
Professor Emeritus
  College of Fine Arts
  University of Kentucky
  Lexington, Kentucky

Deborah Cooper, M.Ed.
Coordinating Director of Arts Education
  Curriculum and Instruction
  Charlotte-Mecklenburg Schools
  Charlotte, North Carolina

Sandra M. Epps, Ph.D.
Multicultural Art Education Consultant
  New York, New York

Mary Jo Gardere
Multi-Arts Specialist
  Eladio Martinez Learning Center
  Dallas, Texas

Carlos G. Gómez, M.F.A.
Professor of Fine Art
  University of Texas at Brownsville
    and Texas Southmost College
  Brownsville, Texas

Kristina Lamour, M.F.A.
Assistant Professor
  The Art Institute of Boston
    at Lesley University
  Boston, Massachusetts

Melinda M. Mayer, Ph.D.
Assistant Professor
  School of Visual Arts
  University of North Texas
  Denton, Texas

Reviewers

Studio Reviewers

Judy Abbott, *Art Educator*
Allison Elementary School
Austin Independent School District
Austin, Texas

Lin Altman, *Art Educator*
Cedar Creek Elementary School
Eanes Independent School District
Austin, Texas

Geral T. Butler, *Art Educator*
(Retired)
Heritage High School
Lynchburg City Schools
Lynchburg, Virginia

Dale Case, *Elementary Principal*
Fox Meadow Elementary School
Nettleton School District
Jonesboro, Arkansas

Deborah McLouth, *Art Educator*
Zavala Elementary School
Austin Independent School District
Austin, Texas

Patricia Newman, *Art Educator*
Saint Francis Xavier School
Archdiocese of Chicago
La Grange, Illinois

Nancy Sass, *Art Educator*
Cambridge Elementary School
Alamo Heights Independent School District
San Antonio, Texas

Sue Spiva Telle, *Art Educator*
Woodridge Elementary School
Alamo Heights Independent School District
San Antonio, Texas

Cari Washburn, *Art Educator*
Great Oaks Elementary School
Round Rock Independent School District
Round Rock, Texas

Critic Readers

Celeste Anderson
Roosevelt Elementary School
Nampa, Idaho

Mary Jo Birkholz
Wilson Elementary School
Janesville, Wisconsin

Mary Jane Cahalan
Mitzi Bond Elementary School
El Paso, Texas

Cindy Collar
Cloverleaf Elementary School
Catersville, Georgia

Yvonne Days
St. Louis Public Schools
St. Louis, Missouri

Shirley Dickey
Creative Art Magnet School
Houston, Texas

Ray Durkee
Charlotte Performing Arts Center
Punta Gorda, Florida

Sue Flores-Minick
Bryker Woods Elementary School
Austin, Texas

Denise Jennings
Fulton County Schools
Atlanta, Georgia

Alicia Lewis
Stevens Elementary School
Houston, Texas

James Miller
Margo Elementary School
Weslaco, Texas

Marta Olson
Seattle Public Schools
Seattle, Washington

Judy Preble
Florence Avenue School
Irvington, New Jersey

Tonya Roberson
Oleson Elementary School
Houston, Texas

Andrew Southwick
Edgewood Independent School District
San Antonio, Texas

Nita Ulaszek
Audelia Creek Elementary School
Dallas, Texas

Tessie Varthas
Office of Creative and Public Art
Philadelphia, Pennsylvania

Penelope Venola
Spurgeon Intermediate School
Santa Ana, California

Elizabeth Willett
Art Specialist
Fort Worth, Texas

Contents

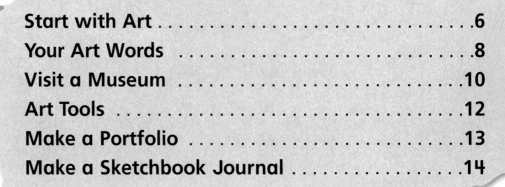

Unit 1

Fernand Léger.
Mother and Child, 1951.

Art in Your World 16

Unit 2

Look at Art **50**

Miguel Vivancos.
Village Feast, 1951.

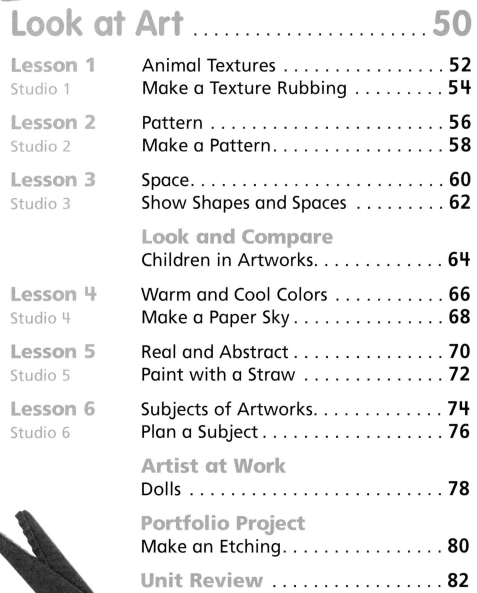

Unit 3

Art Everywhere 84

David Strickland.
Big Bird, 1990.

Paul Cézanne.
Apples and Oranges,
ca. 1895–1900.

Unit 5

Art, Then and Now 152

Vito Acconci.
Face of the Earth #3,
1988.

Unit 6

Art for Everyone 186

Sharon Smith.
Bowl.

Start with Art

Artists make art.
You are an artist.
Your friends are artists too.

Works of art are called **artworks.** Art can grow from your imagination. Look around you. Where do you see artworks?

If you designed your own shoes, what would they look like?

Nancy Graves.
New Year's Greeting.
Silkscreen commissioned by the Jewish Museum, New York.

Bruno Andrade.
A Kinder Place, 2003.
Acrylic on panel, 24 by 30 inches. Collection of Elizabeth B. Reese and Darrell Barger. © Bruno Andrade.

Your Art Words

There are many words artists use to talk about art. You will see some of these art words in your book. They are shown in **yellow.** It is helpful to know these art words when you talk about art.

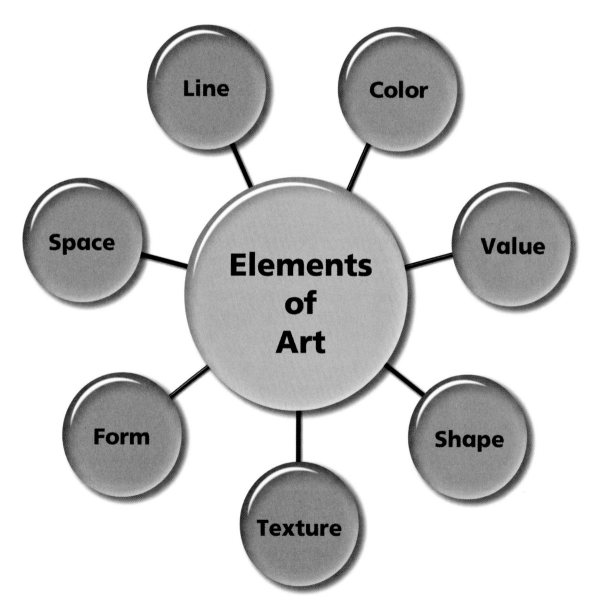

These art words name parts of an artwork.

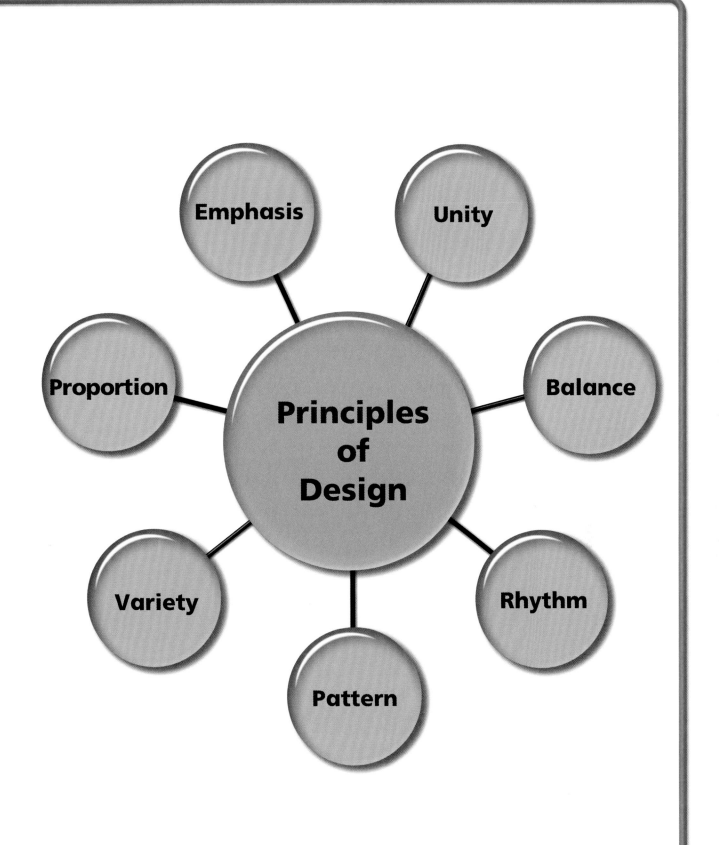

Principles of Design

Emphasis

Unity

Proportion

Balance

Variety

Rhythm

Pattern

These art words tell how an artwork is put together.

Georgia O'Keeffe. *Canna Red and Orange,*
1926. Oil on canvas, 20 by 16 inches. The
Georgia O'Keeffe Museum, Santa Fe, NM.

Visit a Museum

Art museums are homes for artworks. Artworks are displayed and cared for at museums. You can see artworks like this one at a museum. Take time to look at the art. Ask questions about it.

1. What do I see?

2. How did the artist make this artwork?

3. What does this artwork make me think about?

4. What do I like best about this artwork?

Art Tools

Artists use different tools to make different types of art. You will use some of these tools as you make your artworks.

These tools are used for drawing.

These tools are used for painting.

These tools are used for cutting, taping, and pasting.

These tools are used for working with clay.

This tool is used for taking photographs.

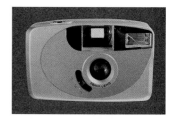

Make a Portfolio

Artists often keep samples of their artworks in a portfolio. Follow these steps to make your own portfolio.

1

Use two sheets of poster board. Write your name across the top of one sheet.

2

Place one sheet over the other. Be sure your name is on the front.

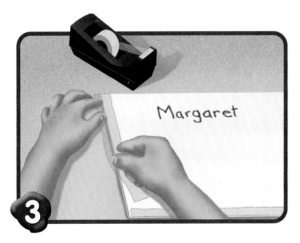

3

Tape the bottom and sides together.

4

Use crayons and markers to decorate your portfolio.

Make a Sketchbook Journal

Artists often use sketchbooks to draw pictures or to write words about their ideas. A sketchbook is an art tool. A small sketchbook idea can lead to a much larger artwork.

Peter Paul Rubens. *Study for Landscape with Cows.*
The British Museum, London.

Follow these steps to make your own Sketchbook Journal.

1

Fold eight sheets of drawing paper in half.

2

Staple the sheets together along the fold.

3

Fold and staple a construction paper cover.

4

Decorate the cover. Write your name on it.

Romare Bearden. *Sitting in at Baron's,* 1980. Collage on masonite, 39⅝ by
29¾ inches. © Romare Bearden Foundation/Licensed by VAGA, New York, NY.

Art in Your World

Art is all around. Art is a green kite in the sky. It is a red flower on a T-shirt. It is a photograph of the moon. It is your own drawing. Art can show how artists feel about people, places, and things. What does this visual artist want to tell you about music?

Meet the Artist

Romare Bearden was an artist, a teacher, and an author. He also liked music. He even wrote songs. What does the artwork tell you about the artist's world? Look for another artwork by Romare Bearden in this unit.

Line

A **line** is like a path. It starts at one place and goes to another. Look at how these lights make lines.

Michael Hayden.
Sky's the Limit, 1991.
Neon. Photograph by
United Airlines.

curved

spiral

thick straight

thin zigzag

wavy

Georgia O'Keeffe. *The Shell,* 1934. Charcoal on laid paper, 18⅝ by 24½ inches. National Gallery of Art, Washington, D.C.

Lines can be straight. Lines can be curved or wavy. Look at the lines above. Name them. What kinds of lines do you see in the painting of the shell?

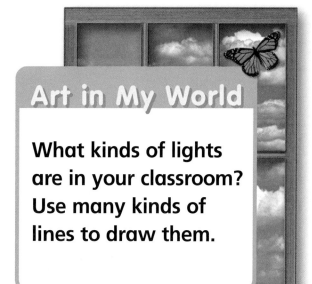

Art in My World

What kinds of lights are in your classroom? Use many kinds of lines to draw them.

Make Lines with String

Follow these steps to make a design
with glue and string.

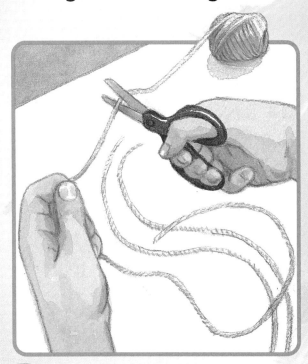

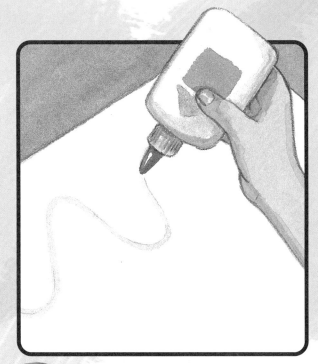

1 Cut some strings.

2 Make lines of glue.

Technique Tip

Glue one string at a time.
Let the glue dry before you paint.

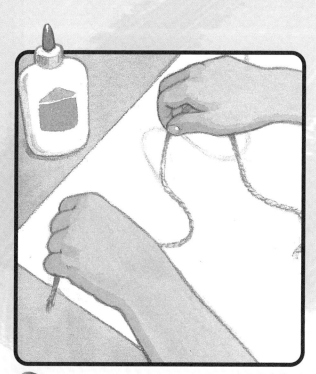

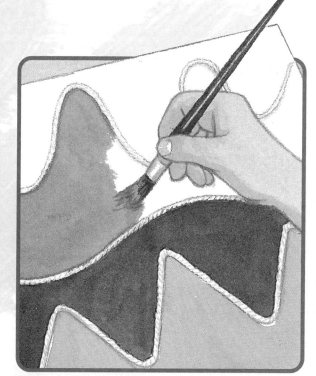

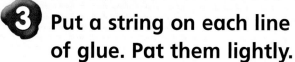 **Put a string on each line of glue. Pat them lightly.**

4 **Paint between the lines.**

Think Like an Artist

Look at the lines you made. Which one do you like best? Why?

Mood

Artists can show feelings. The lines they draw or paint help create a **mood,** or feeling.

Fernand Léger.
Mother and Child,
1951. Oil on canvas,
$36\frac{1}{2}$ by $25\frac{11}{16}$ inches.
The Menil Collection,
Houston, Texas.

Vincent van Gogh. *First Steps, after Millet,* 1890. Oil on canvas, 28½ by 35⅞ inches. The Metropolitan Museum of Art, New York. Gift of George N. and Helen M. Richard, 1964. © The Metropolitan Museum of Art, New York.

Look at the children in both paintings. How do you think they feel?

Name some kinds of lines you see. What mood do they create?

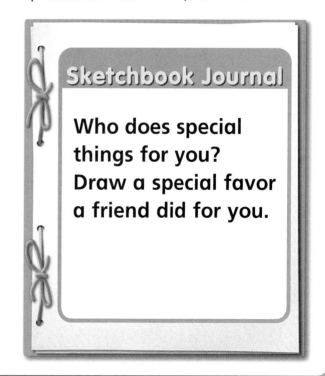

Sketchbook Journal

Who does special things for you? Draw a special favor a friend did for you.

Studio 2

Draw a Feeling

Artists show feelings. Follow these steps to show how you feel.

1 Draw yourself.

2 Look in a mirror. Make your face show how you feel.

Technique Tip

Use crayons to color inside the shapes. Make strokes go side to side. Make them close together.

3 Add lines to make your drawing special.

4 Add something you like to look at or hold.

Think Like an Artist

Name some lines you used. How do the lines show how you feel?

Shape

Artists use **shapes.** Shapes are flat.
Lines can make shapes. Look at this painting
of a parade. What shapes do you see?

Jacob Lawrence. *Parade,* 1960. Tempera with pencil underdrawing on fiberboard,
23⅞ by 30⅛ inches. Hirshhorn Museum and Sculpture Garden, Smithsonian
Institution, Washington, D.C. Gift of Joseph H. Hirshhorn, 1966. Courtesy of the artist
and Francine Seders Gallery, Seattle, Washington. Photograph by Lee Stalsworth.

Look at the shapes.
What shapes can you name?
What shape is the gourd?

You can use shapes to draw something special. You can draw family and friends with shapes.

Sketchbook Journal

Draw some shapes you see. Make some of them touch. Then color the shapes.

Cut and Paste Shapes

Name a pet, toy, or other object that you see. Use paper shapes to make it.

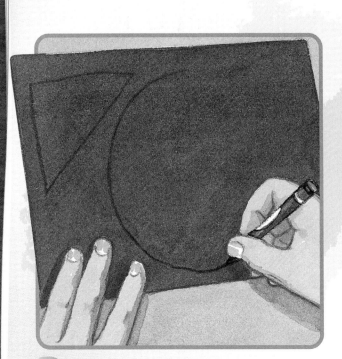

1 Draw some shapes.

2 Cut out the shapes.

Technique Tip

To cut a shape, hold the paper in one hand. Hold the scissors in the other. Cut along the line.

3 Move the shapes around. Make some touch.

4 Glue the shapes the way you like them best.

Think Like an Artist

Where did you put big shapes?

Where did you put little shapes?

Lines and Shapes

Romare Bearden. *Jazz Village*, 1967. Collage on board, 20 by 40 inches.
© Romare Bearden Foundation/Licensed by VAGA, New York, NY.

Every artist has a special way to show
ideas and mood. Look at these two artworks.
How are they different?

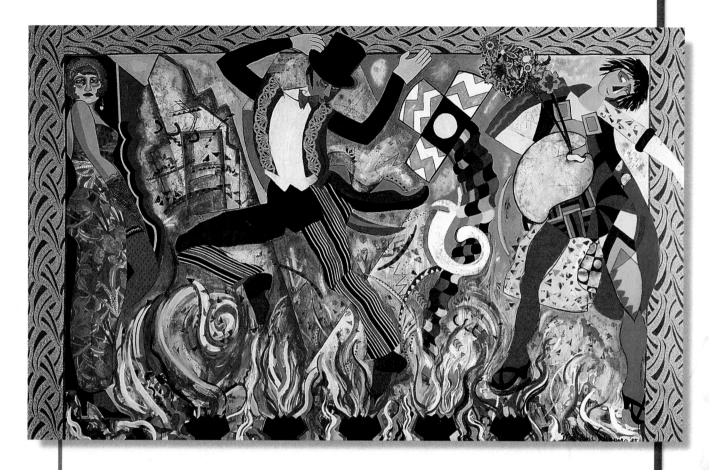

Miriam Schapiro. *Master of Ceremonies*, 1985. Acrylic and fabric on canvas, 90 by 144 inches. Collection of Elaine and Stephen Wynn. Courtesy Steinbaum Krauss Gallery, New York. © Miriam Schapiro.

How is this painting like *Jazz Village*? What kinds of lines, colors, and shapes did both artists use? How did they use them?

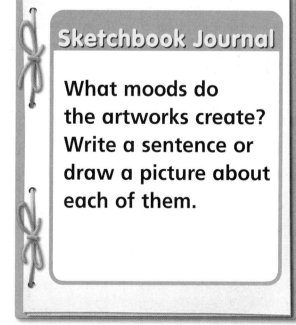

Sketchbook Journal

What moods do the artworks create? Write a sentence or draw a picture about each of them.

Artworks of Families

Artists can show families in artworks. What are family members doing in each artwork?

Carmen Lomas Garza. *Sandía/Watermelon,* 1986. Gouache painting, 20 by 28 inches. Collection of Dudley D. Brooks and Tomas Ybarra-Frausto, New York. © Carmen Lomas Garza. Photograph by Wolfgang Dietze.

Grandma Moses. *The Quilting Bee*, 1950. Oil on pressed wood, 20 by 24 inches.
© 1950 (renewed 1978) Grandma Moses Properties Co., New York.

The artists painted many different shapes. They put shapes together to make new and bigger shapes. How did the artists use shapes and lines to show these families?

Make a Collage

A **collage** is an artwork of shapes. Follow these steps to make a collage of your family.

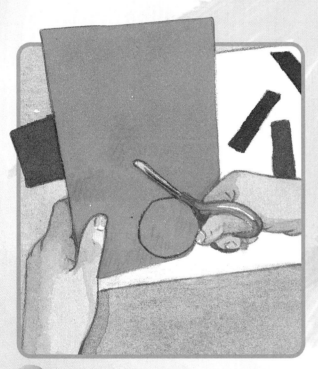

1 Cut out shapes.

2 Move the shapes around.

Technique Tip

To glue a shape, place the tip of the glue bottle on the shape. Make a thin line of glue around the edge. Then turn the shape over and press it on your paper.

3 Glue the shapes on paper.

4 Use scraps for clothes.

Think Like an Artist

How did you make your collage
special? What materials did you use?

Color

What **colors** can you name? Look at *La Piñata*. What color do you like best?

Diego Rivera. (Detail) *La Piñata*, 1953. Mural at the Hospital Infantil "Francisco Gomez," Mexico City, Mexico.

yellow

green

orange

**Color
Wheel**

blue

red

violet

Sometimes artists use color to show mood. Look at the color wheel. What colors might make you happy or excited?

Color can be a symbol, too. What does a red heart stand for?

Research

Look for symbols like green arrows or yellow smiling faces. Draw them. Tell what they mean.

Paint a Symbol

Think about symbols you see every day.
What colors are they? Paint one.

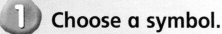 **1** Choose a symbol.

2 Choose a color.

Technique Tip

Before you go to a new color, wash your paintbrush. Then wipe it and blot it.

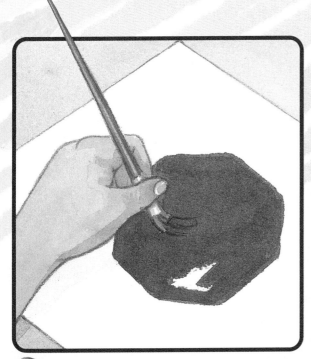

3 Paint the shape of your symbol.

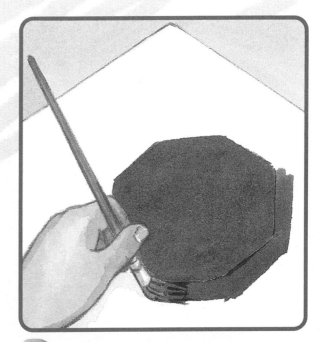

4 Let the paint dry. Then add another color.

Think Like an Artist

What color is your symbol?

What does it stand for?

Kinds of Colors

Red, yellow, and blue are **primary colors.**
Other colors are made from them. Find
primary colors in the artwork.

Morris Louis. *Point of Tranquility,* 1959–60. Magna on canvas, 101³/₄ by 135³/₄ inches.
Hirshhorn Museum and Sculpture Garden, Smithsonian Institution, Washington, D.C.

Artists mix colors. They mix blue and red to make violet. What two primary colors make green? What two primary colors make orange? Violet, green, and orange are **secondary colors.**

Sketchbook Journal

Draw an object you might see on a playground. Use primary and secondary colors.

Mix Colors with Paint

Follow these steps to make new colors from primary colors.

1 Paint a yellow circle.

2 Paint blue in the middle to make green.

Technique Tip

To make violet, mix a dab of blue and red into white paint.

3 Paint a yellow square.

4 Paint red in the middle to make orange.

Think Like an Artist

Look at the colors your friends painted.
How are your colors different?

Murals

Judith Baca designs **murals.** Most murals are really big. They tell a picture story on walls or buildings. More than four hundred children helped paint this mural. It shows the history of California.

Judith Baca

If you painted a mural, what would you paint? Where would you paint it? What story would you tell?

Judith Baca, director; Esabel Castro, designer. (Detail) *1900 Immigrant California, Great Wall of Los Angeles*, 1976–1983. Paint on architectural structures, length approximately 2,640 feet. Photograph by Michael Newman/PhotoEdit.

Portfolio Project

Draw Your Shape

Draw and cut out an artwork of you. Make it as big as you are.

1 Lie down on a sheet of paper.

2 Ask a friend to draw a line around you.

3 Color your shape.

4 Cut it out.

Look at these artworks. How are they
different from yours?

Share Your Art

1. What lines and shapes did you use?
2. What was the hardest part of
   coloring your shape?

Think About Art

Match each picture with an art word.

collage   **symbol**   **secondary colors**   **line**

Write About Art

What kinds of lines and colors are in the cactus above? Finish the lists.

Lines	Colors
curved	green

Talk About Art

- Choose an artwork from your portfolio.
- Tell a friend how you used shapes.

Carmen Lomas Garza. *Hormigas (Horned Toads/Los Camaleones),* 1995. Gouache, 13³/₄ by 18¹/₂ inches. Collection of Ellen Poss, M.D., Brookline, MA. © 1995 Carmen Lomas Garza.

Put It All Together

1. What do you see in the painting?
2. What makes you notice the toads?
3. What did you learn about horned toads?
4. Who would like this painting? Why?

Diego Rivera. *Flower Day*, 1925. Oil on canvas, 58 by 47½ inches.
Los Angeles County Museum of Art, Los Angeles County Fund.

Look at Art

Artists look closely at things all around them. They look at line, shape, and color. You are an artist. You may see shape on a dress. You may see color in a rainbow. What do you see in this painting?

Meet the Artist

Diego Rivera was an artist. His paintings show life in Mexico. They show people working and people having fun. What does *Flower Day* show? Look for more artwork by Rivera in this unit.

Animal Textures

Animals have **textures.** They have textures you can feel. Animals can feel hard or soft. They can feel rough or smooth.

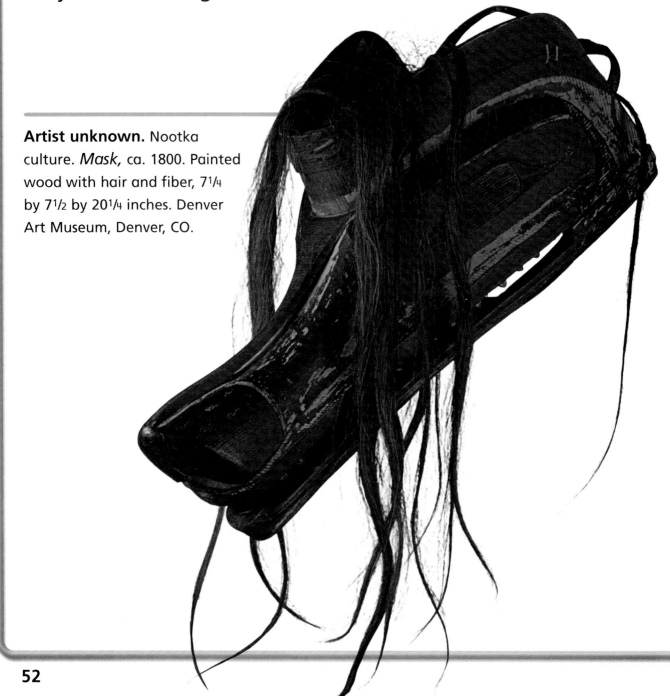

Artist unknown. Nootka culture. *Mask,* ca. 1800. Painted wood with hair and fiber, 7¼ by 7½ by 20¼ inches. Denver Art Museum, Denver, CO.

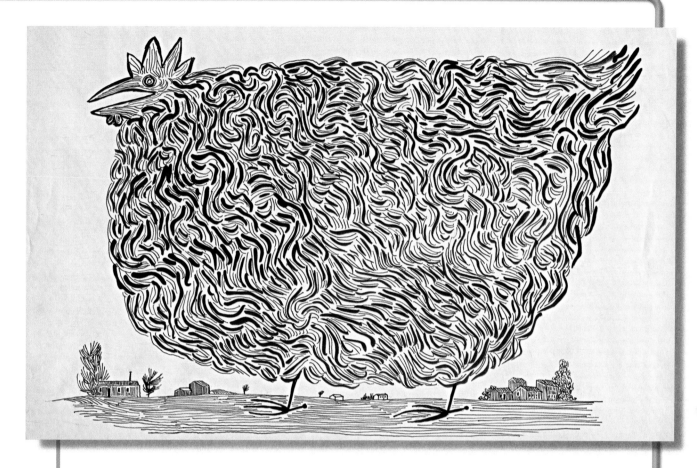

Saul Steinberg. *Hen,* 1945. Pen and brush and india ink, sheet, 14½ by 23⅛. The Museum of Modern Art, New York.

Look at these artworks showing animals.

The artworks show textures you can see. Point to lines and shapes that show texture. Do they look rough or smooth?

Art in My World

Look around you for shiny objects. Now look for dull objects. Shiny and dull are textures, too!

Make a Texture Rubbing

Make an animal with texture rubbings.
Follow these four steps.

1 Rub textures. Use different colors.

2 Cut large shapes from the rubbings.

Technique Tip

To make a rubbing, hold the paper on an object with texture. Rub the side of a crayon over the paper.

3 Move the shapes around. Glue them down.

4 Add lines and shapes.

Think Like an Artist

What textures did you rub
to make your animal?

Pattern

Repeated lines make **patterns.**
Repeated shapes make patterns, too.
Point to patterns in the blanket.

Artist unknown, Navajo.
Blanket, 1880s. Cotton
warp, 83¼ by 60½
inches. School of
American Research,
Santa Fe, NM.

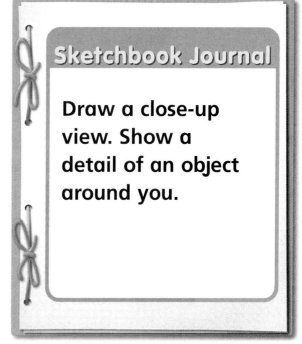

What shape do you see repeated on the moth?

The picture on the right shows a close-up view. Close-up views can help you see **details.** Details are small parts of a whole. Where do you see other details on the moth?

Sketchbook Journal

Draw a close-up view. Show a detail of an object around you.

Studio 2

Make a Pattern

Follow these steps to draw a blanket
that shows pattern.

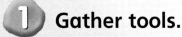

1 Gather tools.

2 Use the tools to
make patterns.

Technique Tip

Use a wide paintbrush to paint large
spaces. Use a thin paintbrush to
paint details.

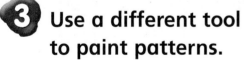 **3** Use a different tool to paint patterns.

4 Draw some patterns.

Think Like an Artist

Name the shapes in your blanket pattern.

Space

There is **space** in front of you and behind you. There is space above you and below you. Look at the painting. What is in the space beside the carousel?

Miguel Vivancos. *Village Feast,* 1951. Oil on canvas, approximately 22½ by 29¼ inches. Musée National d'Art Moderne, Centre Georges Pompidou, Paris.

Look at the girl riding a horse. She takes up space. What is beside her? Point to what is in front of and behind her. What is above her?

Sketchbook Journal

Draw yourself having fun. Show what is beside you. Add something above you.

Show Shapes and Spaces

Follow these steps. Show shapes and spaces around a toy.

1 Draw a toy on white paper.

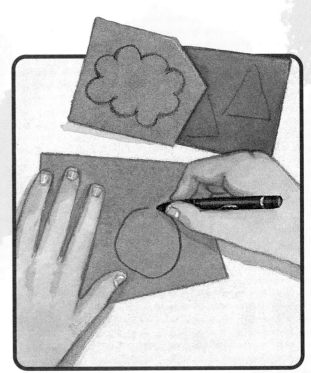

2 Draw shapes on colored paper.

Technique Tip

You can place your shapes above, below, and around your toy.

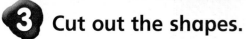
3 Cut out the shapes.

4 Glue the shapes on the page.

Think Like an Artist

Name the shapes you made.

Children in Artworks

Diego Rivera. *Orchard with Children Scene,* 1931. Fresco, 62½ by 104¾ inches. Stern Hall, University of California at Berkeley. Photographed with permission of the Regents of the University of California at Berkeley by Don Beatty © 1983.

Look at these two paintings. Which one seems real? Which one seems like a dream? How else are these paintings different?

Rodolfo Morales. *Tarde de Nostalgia,* 1993. Oil on canvas, 59 by 40 inches. Private collection.

Artists from Mexico created these paintings. Both show people and trees. Where do you see patterns? In what other ways are the paintings the same?

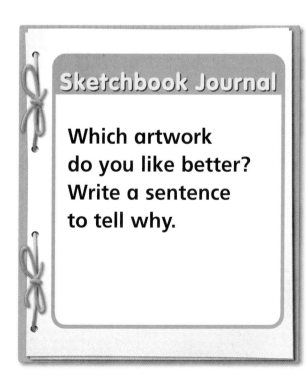

Sketchbook Journal

Which artwork do you like better? Write a sentence to tell why.

Warm and Cool Colors

Which photograph looks warm like a fire?
The colors in the sunset are **warm colors.**
They are yellow, orange, and red.

warm
colors

cool
colors

Which photograph shows green, blue, and violet? These colors are **cool colors.** Artists can use **color families,** such as warm colors and cool colors, to show feelings. How do the colors make you feel?

Art in My World

Look for photographs that show warm and cool colors. Tell how they make you feel.

Make a Paper Sky

Choose warm or cool colors to make a tissue paper sky. Follow these steps.

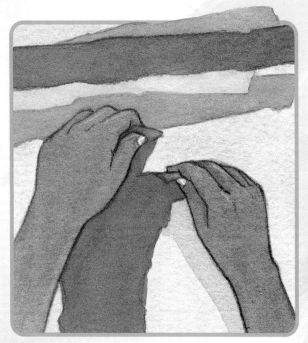

1 Tear tissue paper strips.

2 Brush liquid starch onto the white paper.

Technique Tip

Dip the brush in starch. Start at a top corner. Brush across to the other corner. Dip and brush across again, a little lower.

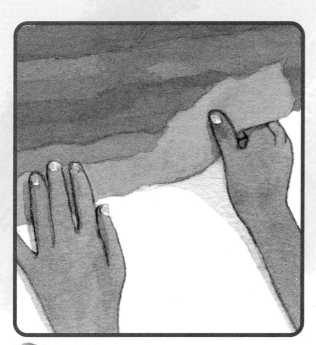

3 Place the strips on the white paper.

4 Cut out black shapes. Glue them in place.

Think Like an Artist

Tell a story about the sky you made.

Real and Abstract

Some artists paint people, places, and things that look **real.** What details look real in the painting of the woman?

Paula Modersohn-Becker. *Old Peasant Woman,* 1905. Oil on canvas, 30¼ by 23⅛ inches. The Detroit Institute of Arts, Gift of Robert H. Tannahill. Photograph © 1996 The Detroit Institute of Arts.

Mark Rothko. *No. 12.* Oil on canvas, 115 by 91 inches. Collection of Kate Rothko Prizel.

Some artworks do not show people or things. Some show only colors. Others show only shapes and lines. These artworks are **abstract.** How would you describe the artwork above?

Research

Look for more abstract artworks in picture books.

Paint with a Straw

Paint an abstract design that shows feeling. Follow these steps.

1 Mix some warm or cool colors.

2 Put a spoonful of paint on the paper.

Technique Tip

Keep the straw close to the paper. But try not to touch the paint.

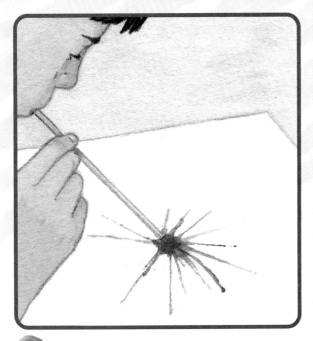

3 Blow through the straw. Keep it close to the paper.

4 Repeat several times with new colors.

Think Like an Artist

What mood does your abstract painting show?

Subjects of Artworks

Each artwork has a **subject.** It is the main idea. People are subjects. Animals, objects, and places are too. Name the subjects in these artworks.

Henri Matisse. *Icarus,* 1947. Color pochoir, 16½ by 10½ inches. New York Public Library.

Frank Romero. *Toto,* 1984. Oil on canvas, 32 by 60 inches.
© 1984 by Frank Romero. Photograph by Douglas M. Parker.

Which artwork shows an abstract subject? Point to a fluffy subject.

Notice that each artist showed the subject so large it fills the frame. How would small subjects change each artwork?

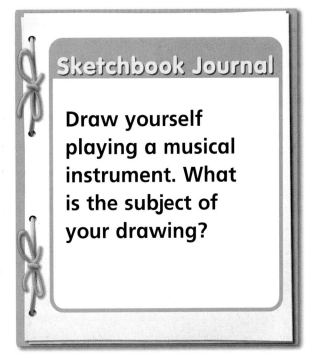

Sketchbook Journal

Draw yourself playing a musical instrument. What is the subject of your drawing?

Plan a Subject

Choose a subject for a collage.
Follow these steps to make it.

1 Choose a subject from a magazine. Cut it out.

2 Glue your subject to the paper.

Technique Tip

Use small amounts of glue at first.
Spread it smoothly. Then add more.

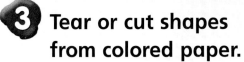 **Tear or cut shapes from colored paper.**

 **Glue the shapes around your subject.**

Think Like an Artist

What do you like about
your collage? Explain.

Dolls

Julie Good-Krüger loves dolls. She collected dolls as a child. Today, she is a doll maker. When the artist makes a doll, she designs a face and picks out eye and hair color. She also decides what the doll will wear.

The dolls on page 79 are made of hard, white clay. What kinds of dolls have you seen? What were they made of?

Julie Good-Krüger

Julie Good-Krüger. *Missy with Big Bad Wolf...Visiting Grandma.* Porcelain, cloth, and cold cast resin. 14 inches.

Julie Good-Krüger. *Nicki with Squirt, Dab, and Scribble... Bright Spots.* Porcelain, cloth, and cold cast resin. 14 inches.

Make an Etching

Use lines, colors, and shapes to make a scratchboard etching.

1

Use warm or cool colors to fill the paper.

2

Cover the page with black paint. Let it dry.

3

Use chalk to draw a subject. Add details.

4

Scratch through the picture. Show texture and pattern.

Look at the scratchboard drawings by other children. What colors do you see?

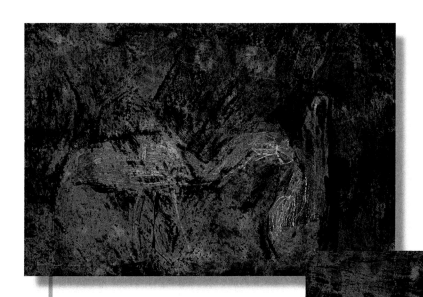

Garrett, Age 6. *Dinosaur.*
Crayon, tempera paint, and chalk.

Brittany, Age 6. *Blue Birds.*
Crayon, tempera paint, and chalk.

Share Your Art

1. What is the subject of your artwork?
2. What part do you like best? Why?

Think About Art

Match the pictures with the art words.

abstract   **real**   **pattern**   **cool colors**

Write About Art

What textures can you see and feel in the classroom? Finish the list.

Textures
hard
soft

Talk About Art

Which artworks in this book are abstract?

Wassily Kandinsky. *Grüngasse in Murnau (Green Lane in Murnau)*, 1909. Oil, gouache and watercolor on cardboard, 13⅕ by 17⅘ inches. Städtische Galerie im Lenbachhaus, Munich. Photograph © AKG London.

Put It All Together

1. What is the subject of this artwork?
2. How did the artist use warm and cool colors?
3. What does this artwork remind you of?
4. Does the artwork make you want to visit this place? Why or why not?

Edgar Degas. *The Little Fourteen-Year-Old Dancer*, 19th–20th century (executed ca. 1880; cast in 1922). Cast by A. A. Hébrard. Bronze, partially tinted, with cotton skirt and satin hair-ribbon; wood base; height 39 inches. Metropolitan Museum of Art, New York.

Art Everywhere

Look indoors. Look outdoors. You can see art in many places. Some art is flat. Some art can be seen from all sides. Look at this artwork. What can you tell about it?

Meet the Artist

Edgar Degas often showed dancers in his artwork. What kind of dancer do you see? How can you tell? You will see another artwork by Degas in this unit.

Edgar Degas. *self–portrait in a Brown Vest,* ca,1856.

Forms in Nature

The object on this page is a **form.** You can go around a form. You can look at it from all sides.

What does this artwork look like?

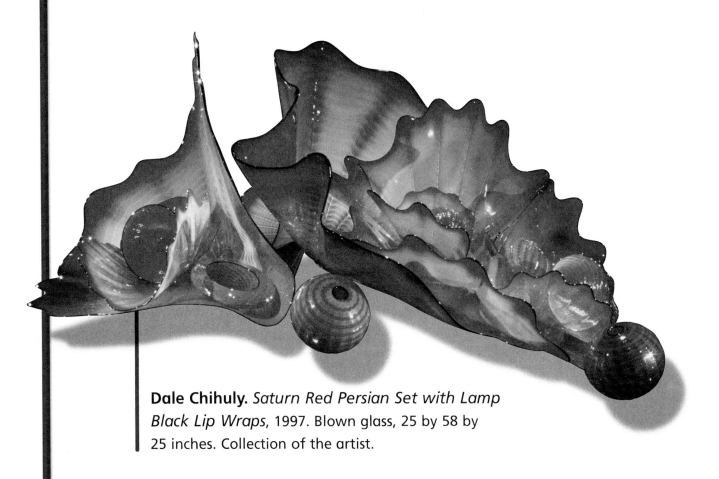

Dale Chihuly. *Saturn Red Persian Set with Lamp Black Lip Wraps*, 1997. Blown glass, 25 by 58 by 25 inches. Collection of the artist.

A **sculpture** is a form. An artist who makes sculptures is called a **sculptor.** Some sculptors use clay, wood, glass, or stone. What did this sculptor use?

Art in My World

Draw pictures of natural forms you see outside. Name them.

Make a Sculpture

It can be fun to use objects from nature to make a sculpture. Here's how.

1 Find small forms from nature.

2 Think of a subject.

Technique Tip

You can connect forms with wire. Wrap and pull the wire. Twist the ends.

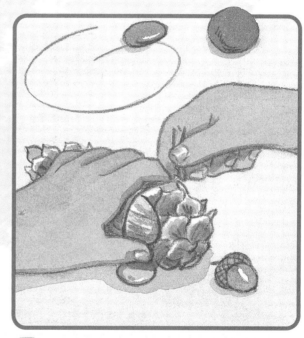

 **3** Arrange the forms.

4 Attach the parts with wire and clay.

Think Like an Artist

What is your sculpture about?

How did you choose your objects?

You Are a Form

These dolls show two artists. They are forms made from soft cloth. The dolls are called **soft sculptures.**

Tani Guthrie and Dran Hamilton. *Frida Kahlo and Georgia O'Keeffe,* 1999. Cloth, 22 by 8 by 5 inches. Collection of Robyn Montana Turner, Austin, TX.

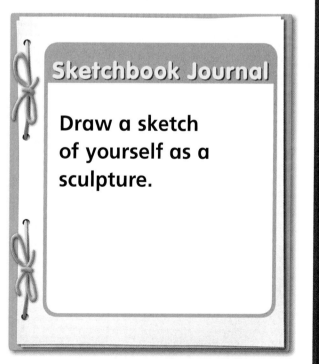

Your body is a form, too. You can float on the water in a big tube. You can fill up a sleeping bag. How would a soft sculpture of you look and feel?

Sketchbook Journal

Draw a sketch of yourself as a sculpture.

Make a Soft Sculpture

How might you look as a soft sculpture?
Find out!

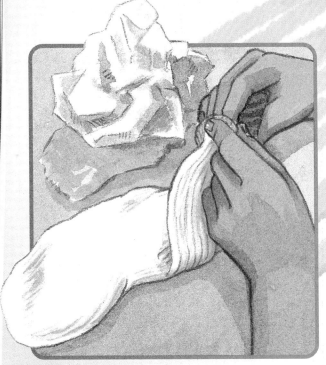

1 Stuff a sock.

2 Put a rubber band around the open end.

Technique Tip

Use markers to draw details on the sock.

3 Cut and glue felt shapes.

4 Add yarn or ribbon for hair.

Think Like an Artist

What details make your soft sculpture look like you?

Found-Object Sculpture

Sculptors sometimes save objects they find. They put them together. Why are these forms called **found-object sculptures?**

David Strickland. *Big Bird*, 1990. Found metal objects and scrap metal, 58 by 52 by 55 inches. Collection of Sally Griffiths, Dallas, TX.

Felix "Fox" Harris. *Yard Art*, various dates. Recycled metal. Beaumont, TX.

Look at both sculptures. Tell what each reminds you of. What found objects did the artists use?

Each artist created an **original** sculpture. It is not like anyone else's.

Art in My World

List or draw objects you have found. Use some of them to draw a sculpture of a funny person.

Make an Animal Form

Clay and game pieces can make a funny animal. Follow the directions to make one.

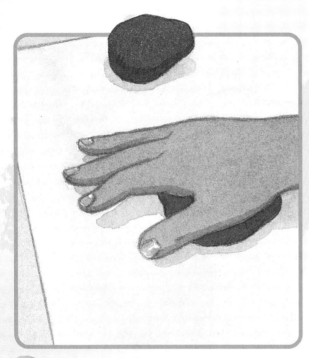

1 Make a head and body.

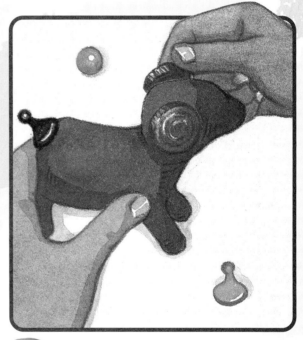

2 Add the face and body parts.

Technique Tip

Sometimes clay is bumpy. Use the tips of your fingers to smooth the edges.

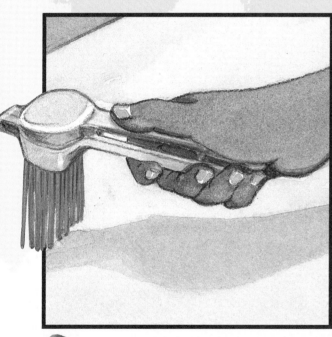

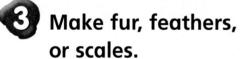 **Make fur, feathers, or scales.**

 **Put it all together.**

Think Like an Artist

Would you change anything
about your sculpture? Explain.

Sculpted Horses

Edgar Degas. *Jockey on a Horse.*
Bronze, 12³/₈ by 9¹/₂ inches.
Private collection.

What is the subject of each sculpture?
Why might artists like to show horses?

Artist unknown, Eastern Han Dynasty. *The Flying Horse,* 2nd century A.D. Bronze, 13½ by 17¾ inches. Photograph © Robert Harding Picture Library.

The horses in these sculptures look real. How would they look if the sculptors had made them as soft sculptures? What materials could they have used?

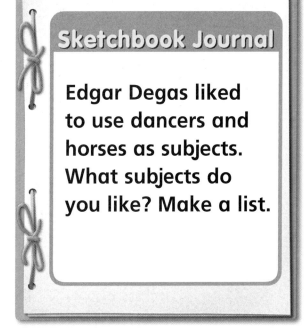

Sketchbook Journal

Edgar Degas liked to use dancers and horses as subjects. What subjects do you like? Make a list.

Movement All Around

Do the children in this sculpture seem to be moving or standing still? How did the sculptor show **movement?**

Glenna Goodacre. *Olympic Wannabes*, 2000. Bronze, 6 by 11 by 3 feet. Sarasota's Selby Five Points Park at Selby Library, Sarasota, FL.

Some artists make lines that show movement. Pictures show movement, too. How can you tell these subjects are in action?

Research

Find another artwork that shows movement. Draw or write about it.

Show Movement

Think about how you move. Make a sculpture of yourself in action.

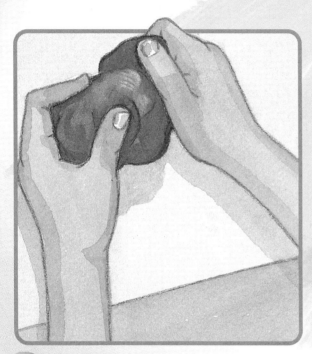

1 **Squeeze and press the clay.**

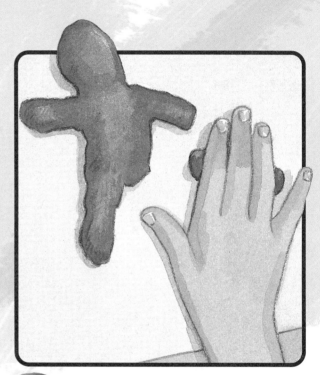

2 **Make your body.**

Technique Tip

Cut the base slab with a plastic knife. Use a ruler to make a straight line.

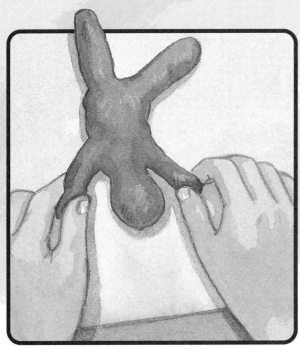

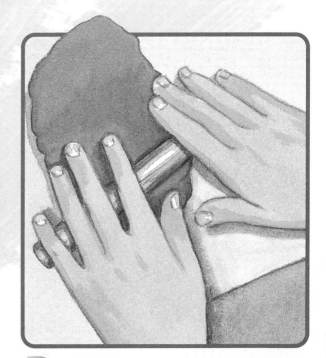

3 Show yourself in action.

4 Roll and cut a slab for the base.

Think Like an Artist

What movement did you show?

Puppets in Action

A **puppet** can show movement. You can make it dance or wave. What else can it do? How? Hint: Look at the strings.

Artist unknown, Burmese. *Puppets*, date unknown. Myanmar (Burma).

Some people tell stories using puppets. They may stand behind a **puppet stage.** When you watch the show, you can see the puppets. Who is hard to see? Why?

Sketchbook Journal

Think about a puppet show you have seen. Draw or write about it.

Make a Sack Puppet

Follow these steps to make a puppet from a paper sack.

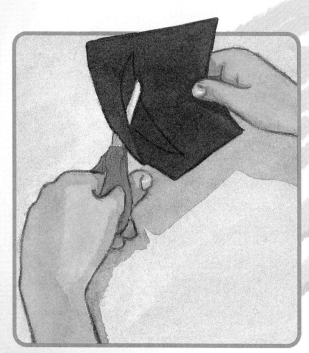

1 Cut shapes for the eyes, nose, and mouth.

2 Glue them to the bottom of the sack.

Technique Tip

Before you begin, plan your puppet. Draw a sketch. Make changes if you wish. Then make the puppet.

3 Add some hair.

4 Draw the rest.

Think Like an Artist

You made an original artwork.

What makes your puppet different?

Mobiles

These sculptures hang from above.
When the air moves, they move, too.
They are **mobiles.**

Alexander Calder.
Untitled, ca. 1939.
Metal, plastic, bone,
wood, plexiglass,
wire, string, and
paint, 24 by 20 1/2 by
3/4 inches. Private
collection.

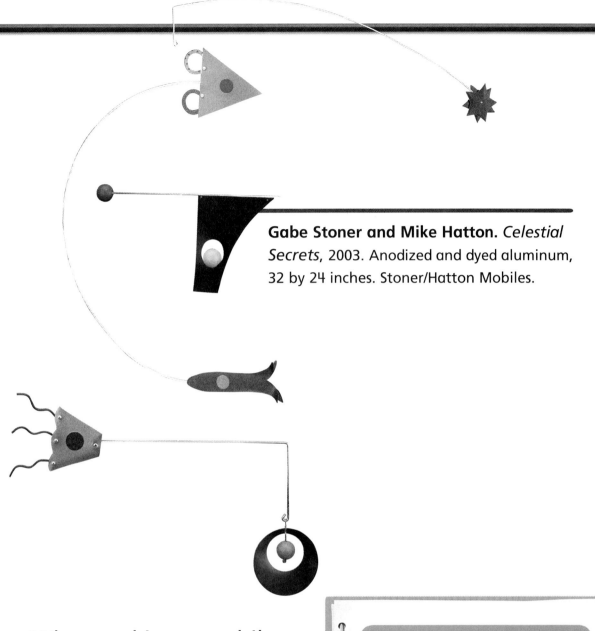

Gabe Stoner and Mike Hatton. *Celestial Secrets*, 2003. Anodized and dyed aluminum, 32 by 24 inches. Stoner/Hatton Mobiles.

When making a mobile, artists use different colors and textures. The parts of the mobile can look real or abstract. The artist can even use found objects. What did these artists use?

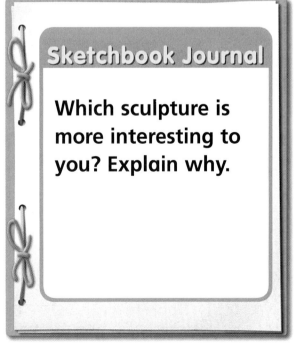

Sketchbook Journal

Which sculpture is more interesting to you? Explain why.

Make a Mobile

Work with friends. Think of a subject for a mobile. Then make it.

1 Cut out a shape.

2 Decorate your shape on both sides.

Technique Tip

Hang the mobile. Then move the shapes until it hangs straight.

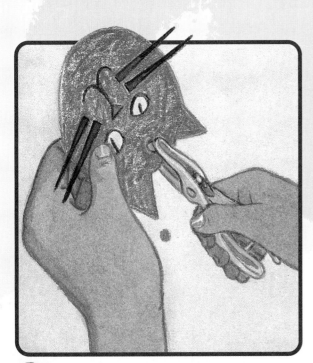

3 Punch a hole in it. Tie yarn through the hole.

4 Add your shape to the others.

Think Like an Artist

How did your group work together to make the mobile hang straight?

Pottery

Patrick Dragon is a potter. He works with clay. He makes pottery, such as bowls and vases. To make his artwork, Dragon puts soft, wet clay on a potter's wheel. As it turns, he shapes the clay with his hands. Dragon bakes the pottery in a special oven to make it hard. What types of pottery would you like to make?

Patrick Dragon shapes a clay pot.

Patrick Dragon. *Humpbacks*. Earthenware clay, 16 inches by 12 inches.

Make a Coil Pot

Some potters use a potter's wheel, but you can make a pot with just your hands.

1 Roll a long piece of clay.

2 Make a coil for the base.

3 Coil more clay on top. Make a lid and handles, too.

4 Rub the clay so it is smooth.

Look at the coil pots these children made. They are original artworks.

Tiffany, Age 6.
Stove Pot.
Modeling clay.

Cecileigh, Age 6.
Handle Pot.
Modeling clay.

Share Your Art

1. What makes your pot original?
2. How did you make the clay softer?

Unit Review

Think About Art

Match the pictures with the art words.

form   **mobile**   **sculptor**   **movement**

Alexander Calder. *Mobile on Two Planes*, Musée National d'Art Moderne, Centre Georges Pompidou, Paris/Superstock

Write About Art

Look at the puppet you made in Studio 5. What part might your puppet play in a puppet show? Write about it.

Talk About Art

- Look back at a sculpture you made.
- Explain how you made it.

116

Artist unknown. *Acoma Polychrome Jar*, ca. 1900.
Burnished cream slip, diameter 13 inches. ©1993 Sotheby's, Inc.

Put It All Together

1. What do you see? Tell about it.
2. What shapes from nature do you see?
3. What do you think the jar was used for?
4. How would you use this pottery jar?

Auguste Renoir. *Girl with a Watering Can.* 1876. Oil on Canvas, 39$\frac{1}{2}$ by 28$\frac{3}{4}$ inches. National Gallery of Art, Washington, D.C.

Think Like an Artist

Artists think about art in many ways. They think about ideas and feelings. They imagine pictures in their minds.

What do you think the girl in this picture is thinking about? What might she be imagining?

Meet the Artist

Auguste Renoir was a French artist. His early paintings show real life. They are filled with color and light. He wanted them to be pleasing. Do you think this painting is pleasing? Explain. Look for another painting by Renoir in this unit.

Auguste Renoir. *Portrait of the Artist*, 1897.

Important Parts

Artists think about how to show what is important. They show **emphasis.** What do you see first in this artwork? Tell why.

Franz Marc. *Die Weltenkuh (The World Cow),* 1913. Oil on canvas, 27 7/8 by 55 5/8 inches. The Museum of Modern Art, New York.

René Magritte.
The Great Family,
1963. Oil on canvas,
39 by 31⅕ inches.
Private collection.

Artworks can show what is important in different ways. It may be a large shape. It may be a bright color. How did this artist show emphasis?

Art in My World

Cut out ads for foods, toys, and cars. Circle what catches your eye. Think about why.

Show Emphasis

What is important to you? Follow the steps to show it in a collage.

1 Find a picture.

2 Cut it out.

Technique Tip

Cut close to the edge of your subject.

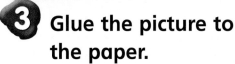 **Glue the picture to the paper.**

 **④ Draw details. Make your subject stand out.**

Think Like an Artist

How did you show emphasis in your collage? Is it pleasing? Explain.

Senses

Artists use their **senses** to see, hear, smell, touch, and taste. You are an artist. What can you learn by touching an object?

Doris Lee. *Thanksgiving*, 1935. Oil on canvas, 28¹/₁₀ by 40 inches. The Art Institute of Chicago, Chicago, IL.

Paul Cézanne. *Apples and Oranges*, ca. 1895–1900. Oil on canvas, 28 9/10 by 36 1/4 inches. Musée d'Orsay, Paris.

Some artists paint about senses. Look at *Thanksgiving.* How are people using senses?

Other artists use their senses to create artworks. Look at *Apples and Oranges.* What senses might have helped the artist? How?

Sketchbook Journal

Draw a snack you enjoy. Write words that describe how it looks, smells, and tastes.

125

Paint with Imagination

Picnics can be a lot of fun. Follow these steps to paint a picture of one.

1 Imagine the perfect picnic.

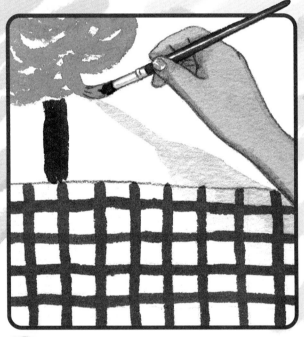

2 Paint a picture of it.

Technique Tip

Look for food pictures that are the right size. For example, a picture of a sandwich should be smaller than the table.

3 Cut and glue pictures.

4 Add people.

Think Like an Artist

What could someone smell or taste
if they were in your artwork?

Balance

Stand on one foot. Put your arms out to help you **balance.**

Artists like you think about balance.

Artist unknown. *Navajo Sand Painting with Theme of Protection,* 20th century.

Look at the sand painting. Imagine a line down the middle. Both sides are about the same. The artwork shows **symmetrical balance.**

Now look at the beetle. Does it show symmetrical balance? Explain.

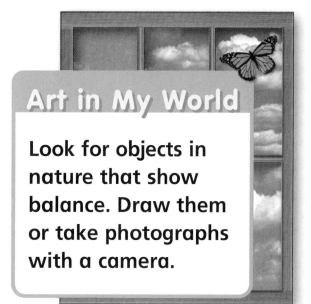

Art in My World

Look for objects in nature that show balance. Draw them or take photographs with a camera.

Make a Blot Print

You can show balance in a blot print.
Here's how.

1 Fold your paper in half. Then unfold it.

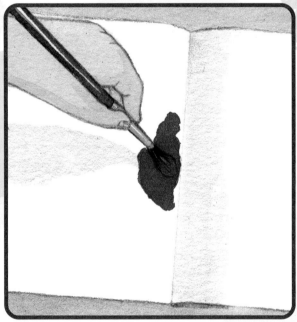

2 Add paint to one side.

Technique Tip

Paint quickly. The paint must be wet when you close the paper.

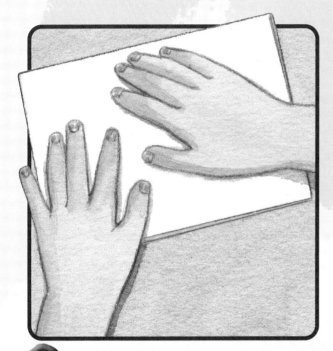

3 Close your paper. Press it together.

4 Open it. Add another color.

Think Like an Artist

Look at your print. What does it remind you of?

Look and Compare

Performers in Artworks

Auguste Renoir.
Acrobats at the Circus Fernando, 1879. Oil on canvas, 52³⁄₁₀ by 39 inches. Art Institute of Chicago, Chicago, IL.

Suppose that you could step into each picture. What are the performers doing? Do you hear music? Which scene has loud music?

William H. Johnson. *Jitterbugs 1*, ca. 1940–1941. Oil on plywood, 39¾ by 31¼ inches. National Museum of American Art, Washington, D.C.

What do you see first in each picture? What leads your eye to the important parts? Tell how the artists used color or shape to show emphasis.

Why do you think the artist showed such large hands in *Jitterbugs 1?*

Sketchbook Journal

Would it be more fun to perform in a circus or dance the jitterbug? Write a sentence to tell why.

Value

Artists use light colors and dark colors.
What kinds of colors did this artist use?

Mary Cassatt.
The Banjo Lesson,
ca. 1894. Pastel on
paper, 28 by 22 ½
inches. Virginia
Museum of Fine
Arts, Richmond,
VA. The Adolph D.
and Wilkins C.
Williams Fund.
Photo by
Katherine Wetzel,
©Virginia Museum
of Fine Arts.

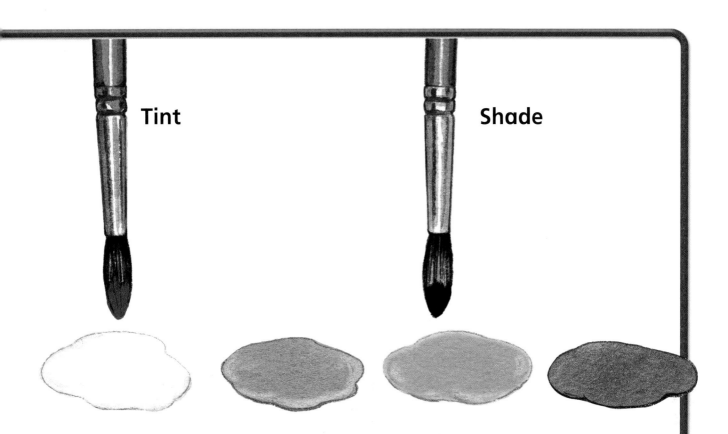

Tint

Shade

You can change the **value** of a color to make it lighter or darker. Light values are **tints.** Dark values are **shades.** How do you make a tint? How do you make a shade?

Find a light blue tint in *The Banjo Lesson.* Point to a dark blue shade.

Art in My World

Look around you for tints and shades of blue. Draw or write about what you see.

Make a Value Collage

Think about dark shades and light tints.
Follow these steps to make a value collage.

1 Choose a color. Tear out pictures.

2 Sort and tear up the pictures.

Technique Tip

Make piles of dark paper and light paper.

 Glue dark paper.

 **4 Glue light paper.**

Think Like an Artist

What color did you choose? What does your artwork remind you of?

Portraits of People

This artwork is a **portrait.** The artist painted a picture of a woman. It shows what she looked like.

Leonardo da Vinci.
Mona Lisa, 1503–1506.
Oil on wood, 30¼ by
21 inches. Musée du
Louvre, Paris.

Vincent van Gogh.
Self-Portrait with Straw Hat, Paris, Summer 1887. Oil on canvas, 15 3/4 by 12 2/3 inches. F469, JH 1310. Rijksmuseum, Amsterdam Vincent van Gogh, Vincent van Gogh Foundation.

This painting is a **self-portrait.** Van Gogh painted a portrait of himself. What does it show about him?

Look at the face shapes in both portraits. How are they different? Draw your face shape in the air.

Sketchbook Journal

Look in a mirror. Draw your face shape with a colored pencil. Draw face shapes of friends. Mix colors to show different tints and shades.

Paint a Self-Portrait

Think about how you look and what you wear.
Follow the steps to make a self-portrait.

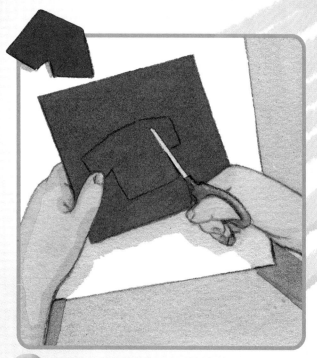

1 Cut out clothes.

2 Paint a self-portrait.

Technique Tip

Mix paints to make tints and shades.
Use the light and dark colors for skin,
hair, and other details.

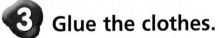
3 Glue the clothes.

4 Paint details.

Think Like an Artist

What does your artwork tell about you?

Does it look like you? Explain.

Shelters

Architecture is about planning buildings. An **architect** planned this house. Why is *Fallingwater* a good name for it?

Frank Lloyd Wright. *Fallingwater*, 1934. Bear Run, Pennsylvania.

Pyramids at Giza

These pyramids are very old. Yet, they still stand today in Egypt.

Pyramids are tombs for kings and queens. Some of these shelters were filled with gold and jewels! How are pyramids and houses alike? How are they different?

Research

Igloos are homes made from ice. Some huts are made from mud and straw. What other materials could be used to build a house?

Make a Clay Pyramid

Practice being an architect!
Follow these steps to make a pyramid.

1 Draw a square. Cut it out.

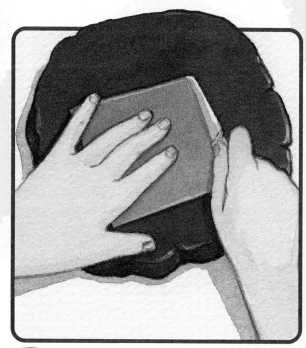

2 Make a clay slab for the base.

Technique Tip

Squeeze and pull the clay to form the pyramid shape. Pinch the clay to make the corners.

3 Add clay slabs for sides. **4** Make a point.

Think Like an Artist

How is your pyramid like the Pyramids at Giza? How is it different?

Toys

Martin Caveza is a toy designer. He designed these toys. Have you played with any of them?

Caveza thinks about what children like to play with. When he has an idea for a new toy, he draws it. Then a special machine makes a model. The model shows the size and color of the toy. He shows the model to the people at the toy company. If they like it, they make the toy and sell it in toy stores.

Martin Caveza

This is a toy designed by Martin Caveza.

Paint an Outdoor Space

Light and dark colors are all around. Use some tints and shades to paint an outdoor space.

Mix some light colors.

Mix some dark colors.

Paint an outdoor space.

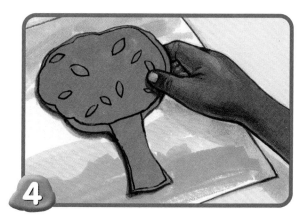

Cut out an object. Glue it on.

What tints and shades did these children use in their artworks?

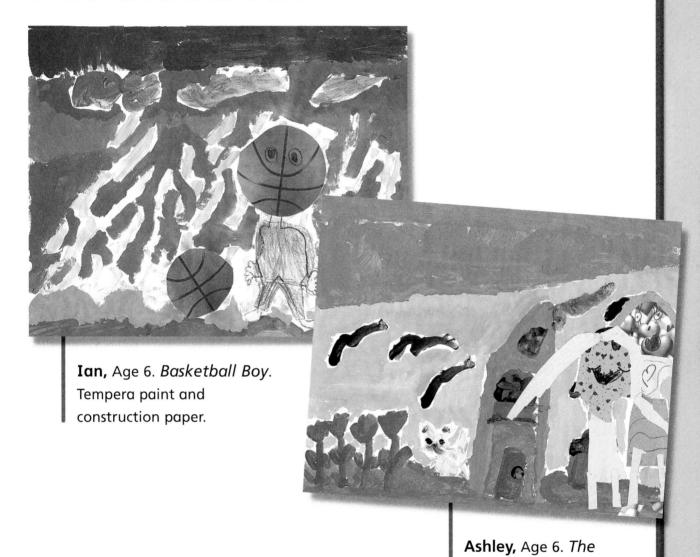

Ian, Age 6. *Basketball Boy*. Tempera paint and construction paper.

Ashley, Age 6. *The Backyard*. Tempera paint and construction paper.

Share Your Art

1. What is the emphasis in your picture?
2. Was mixing tints and shades easy to do? Explain.

Unit Review

Think About Art

Find a picture that matches each art word.

tint **shade** **portrait** **architecture**

Frans Hals the Elder.
A Boy with a Violin,
ca. 1620s.

Write About Art

Suppose you are painting a picture.
It shows you eating a sour apple. How are
you using your senses? Write about it.

Talk About Art

Look at the artworks you made.

- Which was the most fun to make? Why?
- Tell how you used your imagination.

Frida Kahlo. *Self-Portrait (The Frame)*, ca. 1938. Oil on aluminum and glass, 11⅛ by 8 inches. Collections Mnam/Cci-Centre Georges Pompidou, Paris.

Put It All Together

1. What is the most important part in this artwork?
2. How do the frame and face work together?
3. Why do you think the artist painted the frame?
4. What do you think of this self-portrait? Why?

Nam June Paik. *Piano Piece,* 1993. Albright-Knox Art Gallery, Buffalo, NY.

Unit 5

Art, Then and Now

Artworks can tell stories about the past. They can tell stories about now. What does this artwork tell about?

Meet the Artist

Nam June Paik is a video artist. He makes artworks with video cameras. He even uses television screens and music. What do you see on the screens? Look for another artwork by Paik in this unit.

Old Places in Artworks

This painting shows women selling food they made. They are at the Alamo in Texas. The artist painted this mission about one hundred years ago.

Robert Julian Onderdonk. *Chili Queens at the Alamo,* 1900–1910.
Oil on canvas, 12 by 16 inches. The Witte Museum, San Antonio, TX.

The Alamo

This **photograph** shows the Alamo too. It was taken with a **camera.** Does the photograph look older or newer than the painting? Why?

Research

Look at new and old photographs of your community. Tell what changes you see.

Make a Viewfinder

A camera has a viewfinder. It lets you see the view, or picture, you will take. Follow the steps to make a viewfinder.

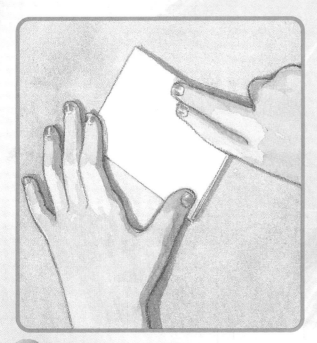

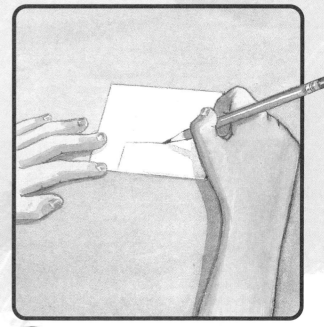

1 Fold the card in half.

2 Start on the fold. Draw a rectangle.

Technique Tip

Look through the viewfinder. Move it to find a picture you want to photograph.

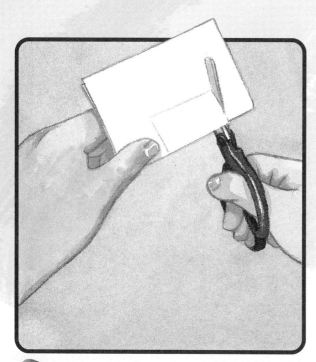

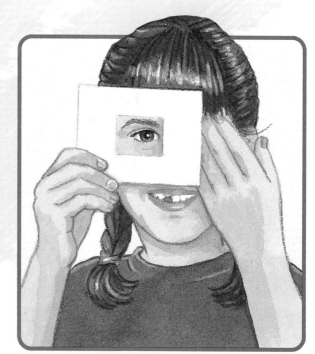

3 Cut along the lines. Unfold the card.

4 Cover one eye. Look through the viewfinder with the other eye.

Think Like an Artist

How can you use the viewfinder to plan a photograph?

New Ways of Seeing

Look at the photographs below. They show **motion.** Where do you see movement?

Still from the animated feature *Monsters, Inc.*

Still from the animated feature *Monsters, Inc.*

Artists can show movement and motion in different ways. Look at the artist in the photograph above. How does she make pictures? How does she make her pictures move?

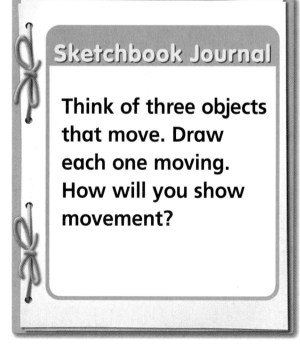

Sketchbook Journal

Think of three objects that move. Draw each one moving. How will you show movement?

Draw Movement

Draw a set of pictures to show motion.

1 Think about how something moves.

2 Draw how it looks at first.

Technique Tip

Before you draw, think about how the object looks first, next, and last. Then plan where to place each drawing.

3 Draw it two more times.

4 Show how it changes as it moves.

Think Like an Artist

What changes do your drawings show?

Storybook Illustrations

Some artists **illustrate** storybooks. Kate Greenaway showed children in her storybooks. She lived long ago in England.

Kate Greenaway. Illustration of "Higgledy, piggledy..." from *Under the Window*.

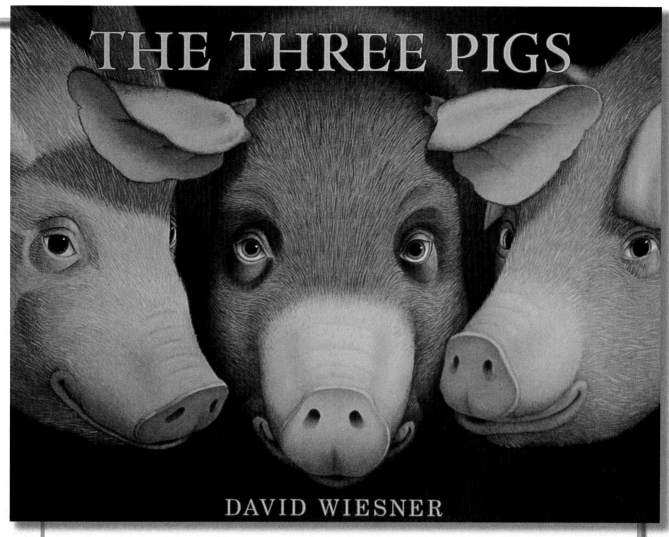

THE THREE PIGS

DAVID WIESNER

Jacket cover from *The Three Pigs,* by David Wiesner, 2001. Clarion Books.

The picture of the children is old. The picture of the pigs is new. How can you tell? What other differences do you see? Does *The Three Pigs* illustration create a funny or serious mood?

Sketchbook Journal

Think of a story you know. How would you illustrate it? List some ideas.

Make a Book Cover

Think of a storybook you like. Follow the steps to make a new book cover for it.

1 Make a sketch of your book cover.

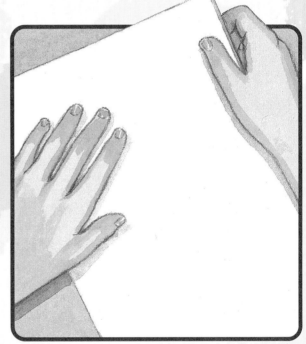

2 Fold paper in half. Draw what you planned.

Technique Tip

Give the cover some texture. Cut shapes from old folders, cards, or wallpaper.

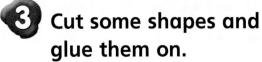 **Cut some shapes and glue them on.**

4 **Add a title.**

Think Like an Artist

Sometimes an artist illustrates the back of a book cover. What would you draw on the back of your book cover?

Old and New Artworks

Artists use different ways to express their ideas and feelings. Look at both artworks. What did each artist make?

Norman Rockwell. *Ben Franklin Signing the Declaration of Independence,* 1926. Oil on canvas, 37 by 20 inches. *The Saturday Evening Post* cover. Printed by permission of the Norman Rockwell Family Trust. © 1926 the Norman Rockwell Family Trust.

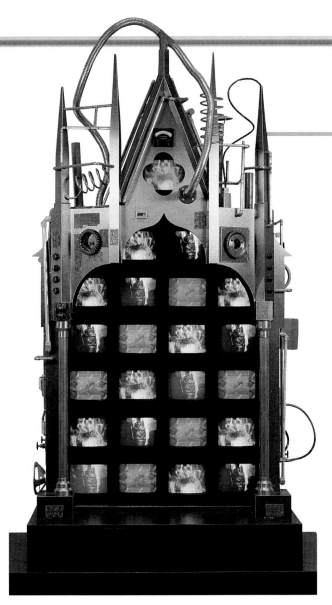

Nam June Paik. *Technology,* 1991. 25 video monitors, 3 laser disc players with discs in a cabinet of various materials, overall 127 by 51 7/8 by 75 5/8 inches. Smithsonian American Art Museum, Washington, D.C.

The artworks of Norman Rockwell and Nam June Paik tell about different times. Which one tells about the past? Which one tells about now? How do you know? Talk about ways the artworks show motion.

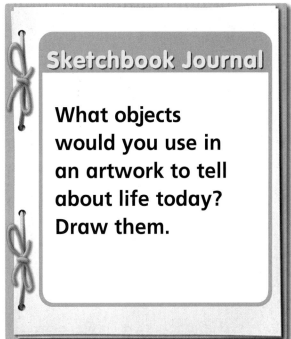

Sketchbook Journal

What objects would you use in an artwork to tell about life today? Draw them.

Messages in Art

A **poster** is a large sign with letters and pictures. This poster was made long ago. How can you tell? What is the subject of this poster?

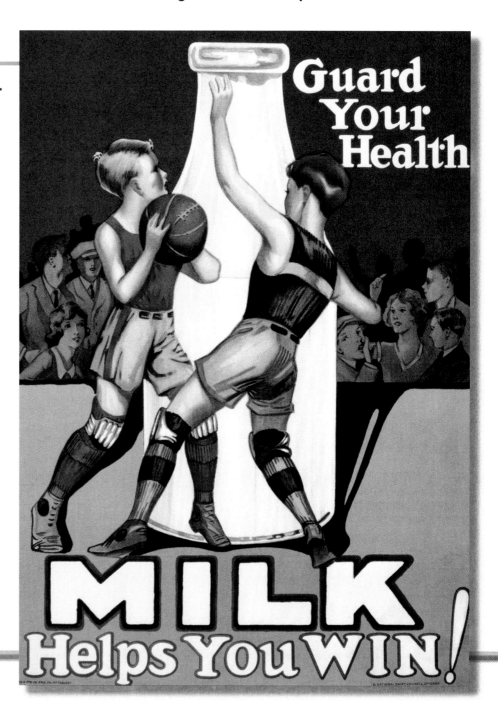

Artist unknown.
Milk Helps You Win! 1937.

A **postcard** is art you can mail. A photograph on one side often shows a special place. The other side has space for a note, a name and address, and a stamp. What does this postcard show? What might you write about this place?

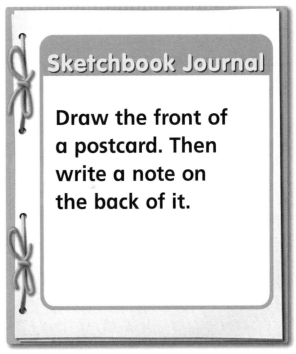

Sketchbook Journal

Draw the front of a postcard. Then write a note on the back of it.

Make a Poster

Think of an event that is happening soon.
Follow these steps to make a poster for it.

1 Plan a poster.

2 Draw your plan on large paper.

Technique Tip

Decide where the paper shapes will go.
Then glue them on the paper.

3 Cut shapes and glue them on.

4 Add some words.

Think Like an Artist

What did you like about making your poster? What would you do differently?

Still Lifes

This artwork is a **still life.** The subjects of the painting are objects that do not move on their own. What objects did the artist paint?

William H. Johnson. *Still Life—Fruit, Bottles,* ca. 1938–1939. Oil on burlap, 21⅛ by 32⅛ inches. Smithsonian American Art Museum, Washington, D.C.

Lilly Martin Spencer. *Still Life with Watermelon, Pears, and Grapes,* ca. 1860. Oil on canvas, 13⅛ by 17¼ inches. National Museum of Women in the Arts, Washington, D.C. Gift of Wallace and Wilhelmina Holladay.

A still life may be about flowers. It may be about food or other objects. Look at both still-life paintings. Which one shows objects that look real? The one on page 172 was made with flat shapes. It does not show objects as they really appear.

Sketchbook Journal

Think of some objects you could use in a still life. Practice drawing them.

Paint a Still Life

Decide on a subject for a still life.
Follow these steps to paint it.

1 Choose three or four objects. Arrange them.

2 First, paint the object that is in the back.

Technique Tip

Take enough time to arrange the objects so they look pleasing.

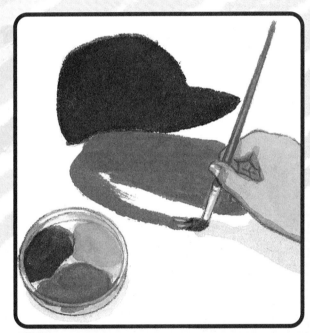

3 Paint the object in the middle.

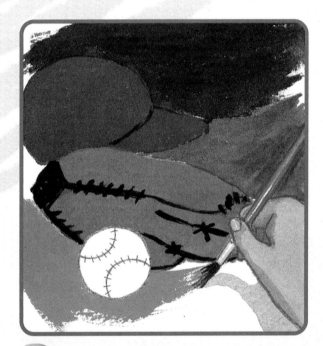

4 Paint the object that is in front.

Think Like an Artist

What does your artwork mean to you?

Public Sculptures Today

Some artists create **public sculptures.** They are in places where everyone can see them. This sculpture is very large. How can you tell?

Isamu Noguchi. *Red Cube,* 1968. Steel with red paint.
Marine Midland Building Plaza, New York.

Vito Acconci. *Face of the Earth #3,* 1988. Concrete, approximately 5 by 33 by 29 feet. Collection of Laumeier Sculpture Park, Saint Louis, MO.

Look at this public sculpture. What does it look like to you? It is made for people to use. You can look down at it. You can go around it.

You can play on the grass around its eyes, nose, and mouth. You can even sit down on its edges.

Sketchbook Journal

Draw a large public sculpture you might create for your neighborhood.

Plan a Sandbox

A sandbox can also be a public sculpture.
Follow these steps to design one.

1 Plan a sandbox. Then draw it on posterboard.

2 Trace each line with glue. Let them dry.

Technique Tip

Touch the tip of the glue bottle to the pencil line. Squeeze gently. Slowly follow along the line.

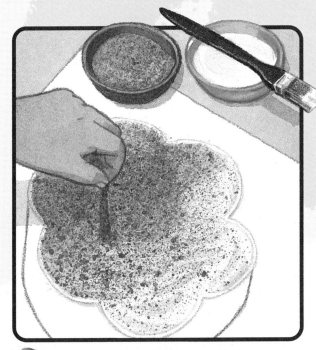

3 Paint glue in the spaces. Sprinkle with sand.

4 Let it dry. Then, turn over and shake.

Think Like an Artist

Look at a classmate's sandbox design.
How is your design different?

Architecture

Paul Williams liked to draw. In school, he often drew animals and buildings. One day a builder saw his drawings. He helped Williams become an architect. Architects draw plans of buildings.

Williams drew plans for homes and churches. He designed schools and other buildings too.

Paul Williams designed more than three thousand buildings.

Paul Williams, architect. *Theme Building.*
Los Angeles International Airport, Los Angeles, CA.

Williams designed this building.
It is at an airport. What does it
look like?

What kinds of buildings would
you design?

Build a Shop

Build a neighborhood shop. Add a sign with pictures, words, or symbols.

1

Paint a shoebox to show a shop.

2

Make a shop window. Show items you can buy.

3

Make a door and a sign.

4

Glue the window, door, and sign onto your shop.

Look at the shops and signs these children made.

Ashley, Age 7. *My Pet Shop.*
Tempera paint, markers, and
index cards on shoeboxes.

Jonathan, Age 6. *Snowboarding
Store.* Tempera paint, markers,
and index cards on shoeboxes.

Share Your Art

1. What do you like best about your shop?
2. What was the hardest part about making it?

Think About Art

Match each picture with an art word.

still life   **postcard**   **motion**   **poster**

Write About Art

How do you know the dog is moving in the photograph above? Explain.

Talk About Art

- Choose a still life from your portfolio.
- Describe it to a friend.
- Tell what makes it a still life.

Alexander Calder. *Flamingo,* 1973. Steel, 53 by 24 by 60 feet.
Federal Center Plaza, Chicago, IL.

Put It All Together

1. What do you see? Read the title.
2. What did the artist do to make you see his artwork?
3. Is this artwork serious or funny? Explain.
4. Where would you put this artwork? Why?

Beverly Buchanan. *House and Garden,* 1997. Oil pastel on paper, 65 by 47 inches. Bernice Steinbaum Gallery, Miami, FL. © Beverly Buchanan.

Art for Everyone

Artists create art for many reasons. They create art in many ways. Some artists make **folk art** about their culture. Folk artists teach themselves. Other artists, like Beverly Buchanan, attend art schools. They may make artworks about their culture, too. Tell about this artwork.

Meet the Artist

When Beverly Buchanan was a child, she traveled with her father. Her artworks celebrate the families and workers she met along the way. What might she want you to see in *House and Garden?* Look for another artwork by Buchanan in Unit 6.

Decorations

The lines, colors, and shapes of the **design** below are made with yarn. It is a **yarn painting.** Some yarn paintings tell a story. What story might this one tell?

Artist unknown. *Huichol Yarn Painting.*

Artist unknown, Fulani culture. *Earrings,* 20th century. Gold, 3¼ inches. Collection of The Newark Museum, Newark, NJ.

Jewelry is artwork you can wear. A necklace, ring, or bracelet can change how you look. It can make you feel dressed up. It can tell about you, too. Look at the gold earrings. Perhaps a woman once wore them. Do you think they would have been worn with a plain outfit or a fancy one? Explain.

Sketchbook Journal

Draw a design for jewelry you might wear. Write about an outfit that might go with it.

Make a Yarn Painting

You can make a painting with yarn.
Here is how.

1 Draw a large shape on paper.

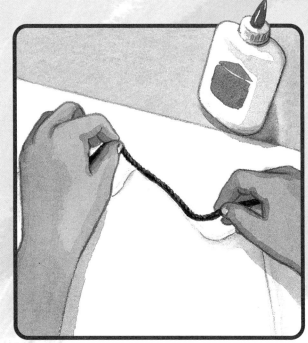

2 Glue yarn along the lines you drew. Let it dry.

Technique Tip

Squeeze a thin line of glue along the pencil line. Place the yarn on the glue line. Cut the yarn to fit.

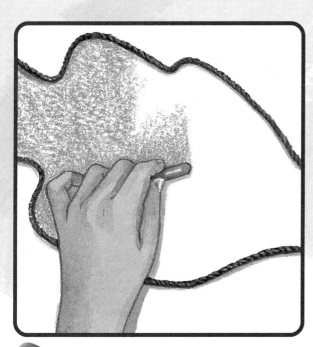

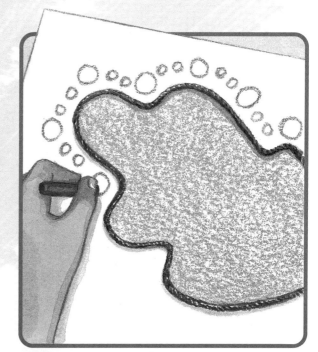

3 Add color inside the shape.

4 Add patterns. Use yarn if you wish.

Think Like an Artist

You made an original design with yarn. What makes your artwork different from your friends' artworks?

Masks

A **mask** covers your face. It can change how you look and feel. What animal does this mask look like? How do you think the artist made it?

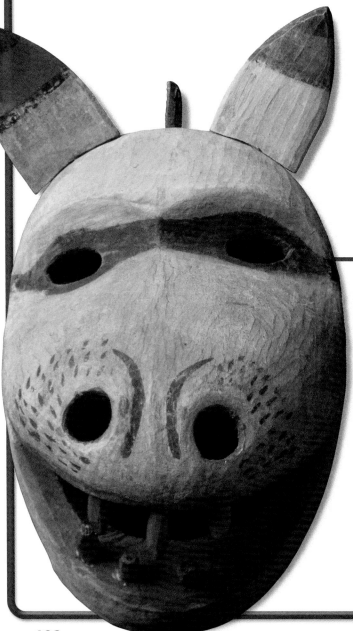

Artist unknown, Kuskokwim River Eskimos. *Wolf Mask,* ca. 1935. Painted wood, separately carved teeth and ears, height 8½ inches. The Newark Museum, Newark, NJ.

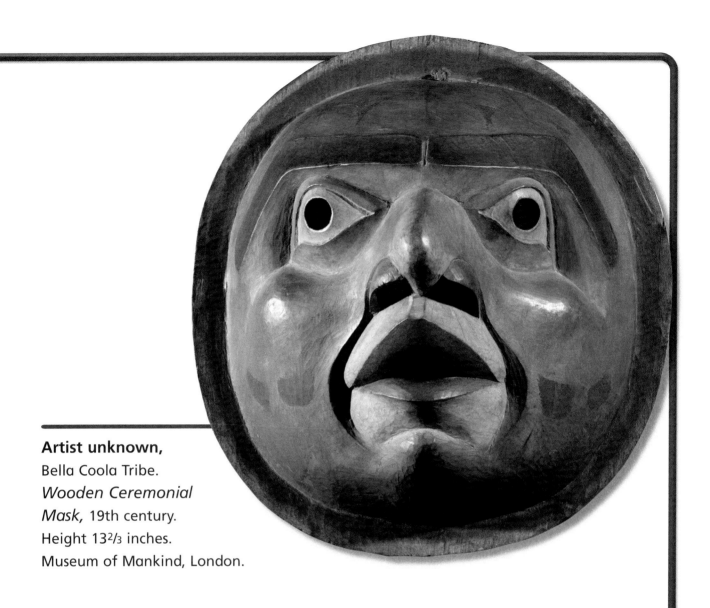

Artist unknown,
Bella Coola Tribe.
Wooden Ceremonial Mask, 19th century.
Height 13²/₃ inches.
Museum of Mankind, London.

How might these masks change how you look, act, and feel?

People sometimes wear masks and dance to music. They may wear them for a special ceremony. When might you wear a mask?

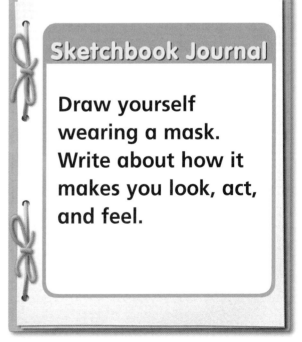

Sketchbook Journal

Draw yourself wearing a mask. Write about how it makes you look, act, and feel.

Cut a Paper Mask

When might you wear a mask? What might
it look like? Here is how to make one.

1 Fold a sheet of
construction paper.

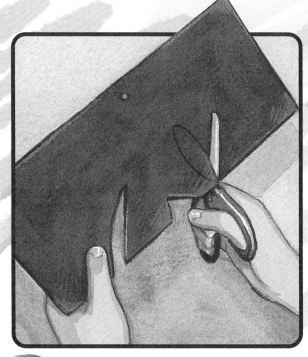

2 Cut into the fold.

Technique Tip

Cut one long oval shape instead of two
for the eyes.

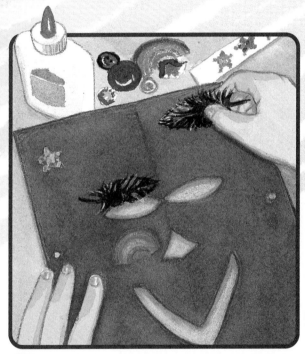

3 Add details.

4 Add yarn for ties.

Think Like an Artist

Does your mask change the way
you look and feel? How?

Special Games in Art

Some artists show special games in artworks. This painting shows a game in an **indoor space.** How can you tell? What special game are the people playing?

Henri Matisse. *Pianist and Checker Players,* 1924. Oil on canvas, 29 by 36 3/8 inches. Collection of Mr. and Mrs. Paul Mellon, Photograph © 1996 Board of Trustees, National Gallery of Art, Washington, D.C. © 1998 Succession H. Matisse, Paris/Artists Rights Society (ARS), New York.

Pieter Brueghel, the Elder. *Children's Games,* 1560. Oil on oakwood, 47 by 64 inches. Kunsthistorisches Museum, Vienna, Austria. Photograph by Erich Lessing/Art Resource, New York.

This artwork is called *Children's Games.* It shows an **outdoor space.** How can you tell it was painted long ago? Name games the children are playing. Point to a game you would like to play.

Sketchbook Journal

Draw your favorite game. Write about whether you play the game indoors or outdoors.

Paint a Special Game

Paint a picture about a special game. Follow these steps.

1 Think about a special game you have played.

2 Paint a picture to show it.

Technique Tip

Use a thin, pointed brush to make thin lines and details. Press firmly on the tip to make thick lines or cover large spaces.

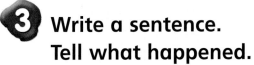

3 Write a sentence. Tell what happened.

4 Write a title. Sign your artwork, too.

Think Like an Artist

Did you show an indoor space or an outdoor space? Tell about it.

Settings

Look at both artworks. Talk about what you see. Where might you see a building like *Flatiron Building?* Where might you see a shack?

Red Grooms. *Flatiron Building,* 1996. Color etching, 34 by 18 inches. Marlborough Gallery, New York.

Beverly Buchanan. *Low Country Shack with Fence,* 1991. Cedar, cypress, pine, nails, and clay, 17 by 17 by 10 inches. Bernice Steinbaum Gallery, Miami, FL. © Beverly Buchanan.

The real *Flatiron Building* is in New York City. It is made of steel, stone, and glass. How do people use buildings like this one?

Look at *Low Country Shack with Fence.* The artist saw shacks like this when she was a child. How is this building different from the one on page 200?

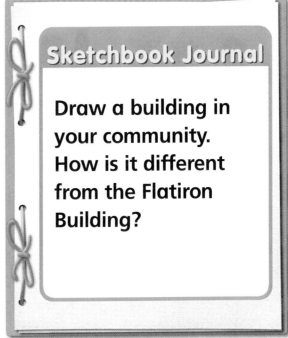

Sketchbook Journal

Draw a building in your community. How is it different from the Flatiron Building?

Fabric Artworks

This artwork is a **mola.** The artist sewed shapes onto cloth with a needle and some thread. What do you see? Tell about the colors, shapes, and patterns.

Artist unknown, Panamanian. *Mola.* 20th century. Cotton cloth with thread. Private collection.

Artist unknown, Peruvian. *Arpillera.* Cloth with yarn and thread, 17 by 19½ inches. Private collection.

This is an **arpillera** (ar-pea-yair-ah). It is a colorful wall hanging. Artists cut pieces of cloth and sew them together. Then they use a needle and thread to add details. An arpillera can tell a story about life. What story might this one tell?

Art in My World

Look for wall hangings and blankets whose designs and patterns tell a story.

Cut and Paste Patterns

Think of a subject for a mola design.
Then follow these directions to make it.

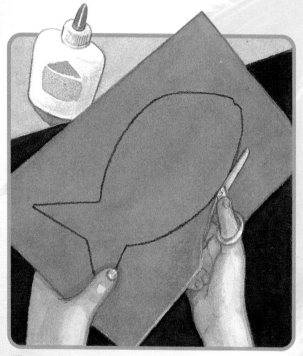

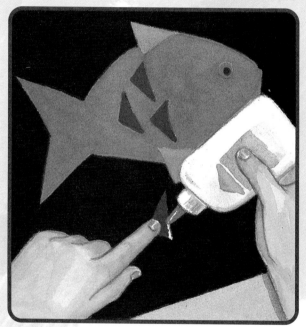

1 Draw and cut out a large shape. Glue it onto black paper.

2 Cut out shapes to show details. Glue them on the large shape.

Technique Tip

In Step 3, cut rectangles. Then cut off each sharp corner. Turn the scissors as you cut.

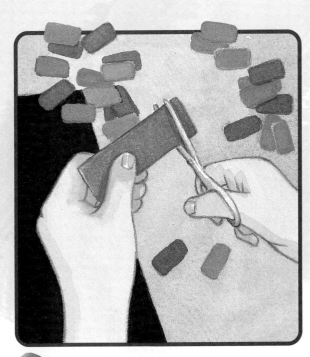

3 Cut colored paper into small rectangles. Round the corners.

4 Glue groups of small rectangles to fill the background.

Think Like an Artist

What colors did you repeat in your mola?

Artworks You Can Use

Some artists make **useful art.**
It is art you can use. An artist made
these salt and pepper shakers.
How are they useful?

Artist unknown, Nepal. *Salt and Pepper Shakers in the Likeness of Frida Kahlo and Diego Rivera.* Painted ceramic, each approximately 3 by 6 by 1 inches. Private collection.

Sharon Smith. *Ceramic Bowl.*
Clay with glazes, diameter 10 inches.
Private collection.

An artist made this bowl. It is useful art, too. Talk about it. Tell about the design. How would you use the bowl in your house?

Sketchbook Journal

Draw a useful item in your house on one side of your paper. Draw a plan for making it look special on the other side.

Make a Clay Frame

Follow the steps to make a
clay picture frame you can use.

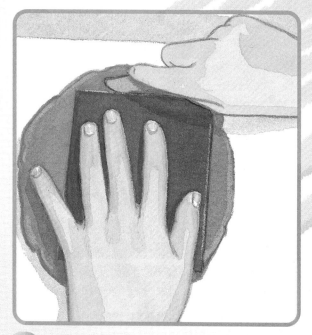

1 Roll a slab of clay. Cut
out a rectangle.

2 Cut a smaller rectangle
from the middle.

Technique Tip

Lay a cardboard rectangle on the clay.
Cut close to the edge of the cardboard.

③ Decorate the frame with small clay shapes.

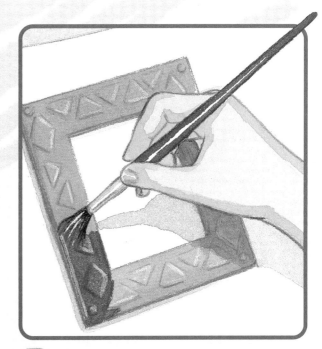

④ Let the clay dry. Paint the picture frame.

Think Like an Artist

How is your clay frame artful?

How is it useful?

Signs and Symbols

Artists sometimes use symbols in artworks. The symbols may stand for a word, a message, or an idea. What symbols do you see in this artwork?

Ida Rittenberg Kohlmeyer. *Signs and Symbols,* 1984. Mixed media on canvas, 60 by 42 inches. Ogden Museum of Southern Art, University of New Orleans.

Signs can help you understand what is around you. Symbols on signs take the place of words. What do the symbols on these signs mean?

Look at the computer screen. The symbols are called icons. Which icon would you click on to go to the next screen?

Art Fact

X is a very old symbol. It has even been found on cave drawings. Today, X on a sign or letter may stand for a kiss.

Make a Sign Rubbing

It is fun to make a sign rubbing.
Here is what to do.

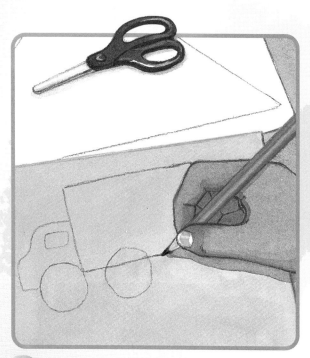

1 Think of a message for a sign. Draw symbols for it.

2 Cut out the sign. Then glue colored shapes.

Technique Tip

Start with the largest shape when you glue. End with the smaller shapes.

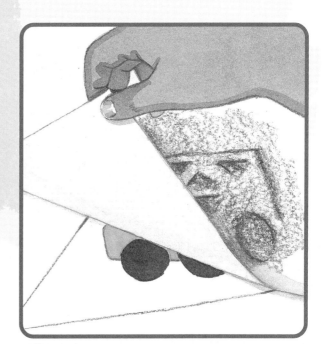

3 Cover with newsprint. Rub the side of a crayon over it.

4 Display your picture and your rubbing.

Think Like an Artist

What message does your artwork send?

Woven Blankets

Clarissa Hudson is a weaver. She weaves yarn and other materials into blankets. She makes the yarn herself. She twists together wool and bark from a tree.

To make a weaving, she first draws a design. Next, she prepares the loom. The loom holds the yarn while she weaves. When everything is ready, she begins to weave her designs into a blanket. Are you a weaver? Talk about your ideas for weaving.

Clarissa Hudson

Clarissa Hudson. *Copper Woman Regalia,* 2000. Wool, cedar bark, copper thread, copper cones, abalone shell, ermine skins. Anchorage Museum of History and Art.

Make a Sign Pendant

Think of a design for a small sign or icon.
You can make it and wear it!

1 Draw and cut out shapes.
Color or paint them.

2 Glue them together.
Let them dry.

3 Make a hole near an outside edge.

4 Use yarn to hang the pendant around your neck.

How would you use the sign pendants these children made?

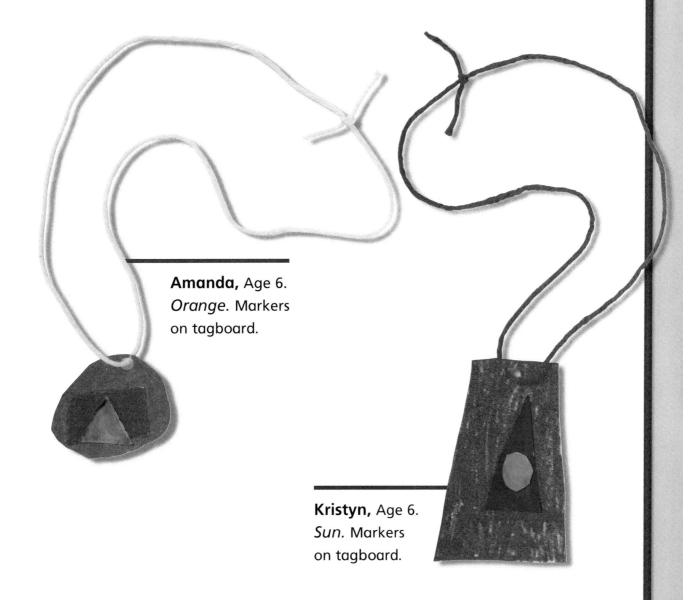

Amanda, Age 6. *Orange.* Markers on tagboard.

Kristyn, Age 6. *Sun.* Markers on tagboard.

Share Your Art

1. How did you decide what design to make?
2. How does wearing your pendant make you feel?

Think About Art

Match each art word with a picture.

jewelry folk art mask symbol

Write About Art

Choose a picture above that shows useful art.
Write about how you would use it.

Talk About Art

- Choose an artwork you created that
  has a design.
- Explain what it is and how you made it.

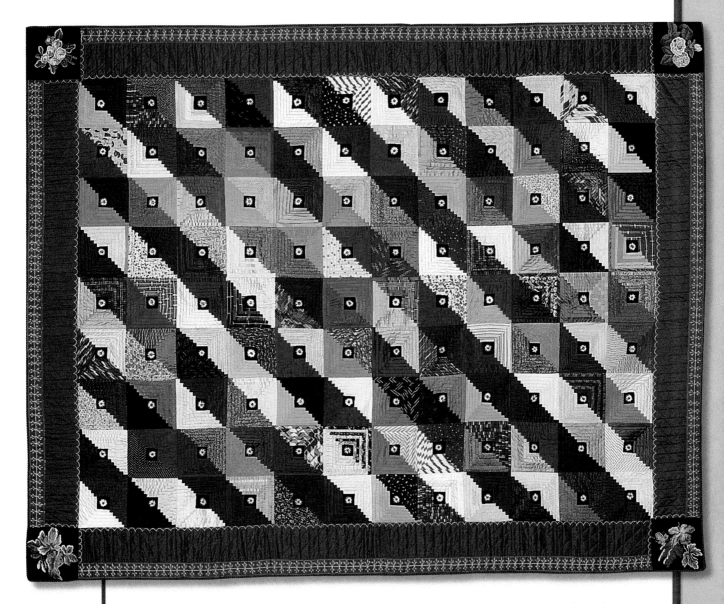

Artist unknown. *Log Cabin,* late 19th century. Coverlet, silk, handmade patchwork, 80 by 63 inches. Courtesy of The Witte Museum, San Antonio, TX.

Put It All Together

1. What do you see? Tell about it.
2. What do you think it was used for?
3. Why do you think it was called *Log Cabin?*
4. How would you use *Log Cabin?*

Elements of Art

Line

straight

curved

zigzag

thin

thick

broken

Color

cool

warm

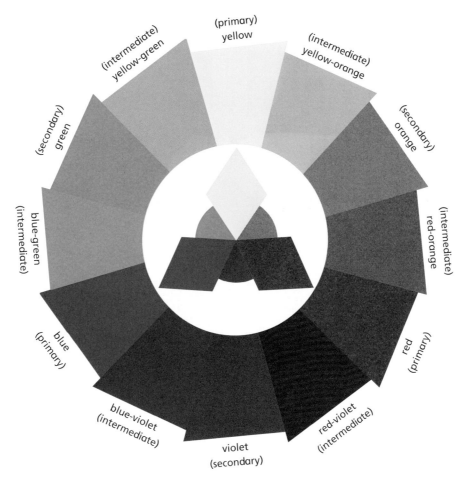

(primary)
yellow

(intermediate)
yellow-orange

(secondary)
orange

(intermediate)
red-orange

red
(primary)

red-violet
(intermediate)

violet
(secondary)

blue-violet
(intermediate)

blue
(primary)

blue-green
(intermediate)

(secondary)
green

(intermediate)
yellow-green

color wheel

Value

Shape

geometric shapes | organic shapes

223

Texture

bumpy

soft

shiny

prickly

sticky

fluffy

Form

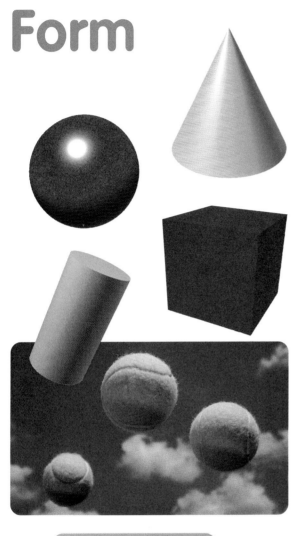

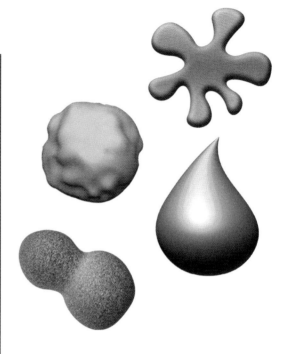

geometric forms | organic forms

Space

positive space

negative space

Unity

Variety

Emphasis

Balance

Proportion

Pattern

Rhythm

Think Safety

Read these safety rules. Be sure to follow these rules when you create artworks.

1. Keep art materials away from your mouth.

2. Keep art materials away from your eyes.

3. Do not breathe chalk dust or art sprays.

4. Look for the word *nontoxic* on labels. This means the materials are safe to use.

5. Always use safety scissors. Take care with all sharp objects.

6. Use only unused meat trays and egg cartons.

7. Wash your hands when you finish an artwork.

8. Get help from your teacher if you have a problem.

Can you think of more ways to be safe?

List of Artists

Unknown Artists

Artists

List of Artists

Picture Glossary

abstract
page 71

architect
page 142

architecture
page 142

arpillera
page 203

Artist unknown, Peruvian. *Arpillera.*

icon
page 211

illustrate
page 162

imagine
page 119

indoor space
page 196

Doris Lee. *Thanksgiving*, 1935.

jewelry
page 189

Artist unknown. *Berber Necklace.*

lines
page 18

mask
page 192

mobile
page 108

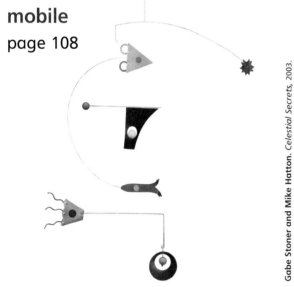

mola
page 202

mood
page 22

motion
page 158

movement
page 100

mural
page 44

original
page 95

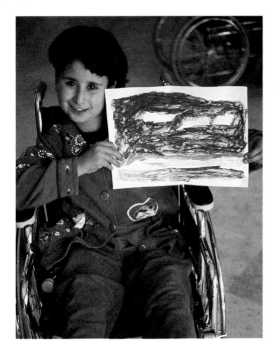

outdoor space
page 197

pattern
page 56

photograph
page 155

portrait
page 138

Leonardo da Vinci. *Mona Lisa*, 1503–1506.

primary colors
page 40

public sculpture
page 176

Isamu Noguchi. *Red Cube*, 1968.

postcard
page 169

poster
page 168

puppet
page 104

puppet stage
page 105

R

real
page 70

Edward Hopper. *Route 6 Eastham*, 1941.

S

sculptor
page 87

sculpture
page 87

Artist unknown. *The Flying Horse*. A.D. 2nd Century.

secondary colors
page 41

self-portrait
page 139

Vincent van Gogh. *Self-Portrait with Straw Hat*. 1887.

senses
page 124

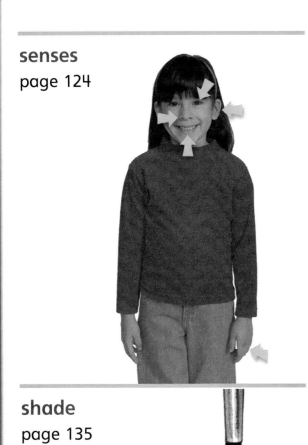

shade
page 135

shapes
page 26

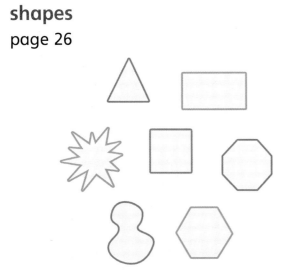

sign
page 211

soft sculpture
page 90

space
page 60

still life
page 172

subject
page 74

symmetrical balance
page 129

Lois Ehlert. *Color Zoo*, 1990.

texture
page 52

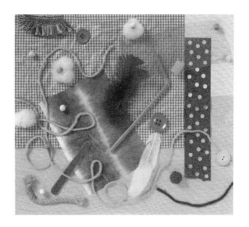

tint
page 135

useful art
page 206

value
page 135

warm colors
page 66

yarn painting
page 188

Index

Index

Acknowledgments

ILLUSTRATIONS

20, 21, 24, 25, 28, 29, 34, 35, 38, 39, 41, 42, 43, 54, 55, 58, 59, 62, 63, 68, 69, 72, 73, 76, 77, 82, 87, 88, 89, 92, 93, 96, 97, 102, 103, 106, 107, 110, 111, 122, 123, 126, 127, 130, 131, 135, 136, 137, 140, 141, 144, 145, 156, 157, 160, 161, 164, 165, 170, 171, 174, 175, 178, 179, 190, 191, 194, 195, 198, 199, 204, 205, 208, 209, 212, 213, 218, 240(cl), 240 (bl), 241, 245, 246, 247(cl) 247(cr), 248 Anni Matsick

46, 80, 114, 148, 182, 216 Linda Hill Griffith

61 James Effler

211 Matt Lemmons

240(tl) Renee Graef

242, 247(tl) Meredith Johnson

PHOTOGRAPHS

Every effort has been made to secure permission and provide appropriate credit for photographic material. The publisher deeply regrets any omission and pledges to correct errors called to its attention in subsequent editions.

Unless otherwise acknowledged, all photographs are the property of Scott Foresman, a division of Pearson Education.

Photo locators denoted as follows: Top (t), Center (c), Bottom (b), Left (l), Right (r), Background (Bkgd)

Front Matter

Page iv (bl), The Menil Collection, Houston, Texas. © Estate of Fernand Léger/Artists Rights Society (ARS), NY; 3(b), Musée d'Orsay, Paris/Lauros-Giraudon, Paris/SuperStock; 4, Collection of Ellen Poss, M.D., Brookline, MA. Photo by M. Lee Fatherree, courtesy, Carmen Lomas Garza; 7(tr), The Jewish Museum of New York/Art Resource, NY; 7(b), Christie's Images/SuperStock. © 2004 Artists Rights Society (ARS), New York/ADAGP, Paris; 10; Georgia O'Keeffe Museum, Santa Fe/Art Resource, NY. © 2004 The Georgia O'Keeffe Foundation/Artists Rights Society (ARS), New York; 14, By kind permission of The Lord Chamberlain's Office, image supplied by The Trustees of the British Museum.

Units 1–6

Page 16, Courtesy of David C. Driskell; 17, Courtesy of VAGA, NY; 18, 1987 United Airlines Terminals, O'Hare International Airport, Chicago. Neon tubes and mirrors, controlled by computers. Courtesy United Airlines; 19, Burstein Collection/Corbis. © 2004 The Georgia O'Keeffe Foundation/Artists Rights Society (ARS), New York; 22, The Menil Collection, Houston, Texas. © Estate of Fernand Léger/Artists Rights Society (ARS), NY; 23, The Metropolitan Museum of Art, New York. Gift of George N. and Helen M. Richard, 1964 (64.165.2). © 1982 by The Metropolitan Museum of Art, New York; 26, Photograph by Lee Stalsworth. © 2004 Jacob Lawrence Foundation/Artists Rights Society (ARS), New York; 27, © Marianne Haas/Corbis; 32, © 1986 Carmen Lomas Garza; 33, Grandma Moses: The Quilting Bee. Copyright © 1950 (renewed 1978)/Grandma Moses Properties Co., New York; 36, © Schalkwijk/Art Resource, NY. © Fiduciario en el Fideicomiso relativo a los Museos Diego Rivera y Frida Kahlo. Reproduction authorized by the Bank of Mexico, Mexico City; 40, Hirshhorn Museum and Sculpture Garden, Smithsonian Institution, Gift of Joseph H. Hirshhorn, 1966. Photo by Lee Stalsworth; 44(t), © Kenna Love; 44 (tr) © Kenna Love; 44-45(b), Photo courtesy of SPARC (www.sparcmurals.org); 48, © Darrell Gulin/Corbis; 48, © Santokh Kochar/ Getty Images; 49, Photo by M.Lee Fatherree, courtesy of Carmen Lomas Garza; 50, Photograph © 2005 Museum Associates/ LACMA. © Fiduciario en el Fideicomiso relativo a los Museos Diego Rivera y Frida Kahlo. Reproduction authorized by the Bank of Mexico, Mexico City; 51, © Bettmann/Corbis; 51, © Jess Alford/Getty Images; 52, Denver Art Museum Collection, Native Arts Acquisition Fund, 1949.3642. © Photo provided by the Denver Art Museum. All rights reserved; 53, Digital image © The Museum of Modern Art/Licensed by Scala/Art Resource, NY; 56, Catalog Number SAR.1999-9-114/School of American Research; © Gary W. Carter/Corbis; 57(cr), © Robyn Montana Turner; 64, Photo © Don Beatty. © Fiduciario en el Fideicomiso relativo a los Museos Diego Rivera y Frida Kahlo. Reproduction authorized by the Bank of Mexico, Mexico City; 66, © Wolfgang Kaehler/Corbis; 67, © Shaffer/Smith/SuperStock; 71, Art Resource, NY. © Mark Rothko/Artists Rights Society (ARS), NY; 74, New York Public Library/Art Resource, NY. © 2004 Succession H. Matisse, Paris/Artists Rights Society (ARS), New York; 82, © Arte & Immagini srl/Corbis; 82, © ThinkStock/SuperStock; © 2004 Wassily Kandinsky/Artists Rights Society (ARS), New York; 84, © Christie's Images/SuperStock; 85(l), Edgar Degas. *Self-Portrait in a Brown Vest*, ca. 1856. Oil on paper,

Acknowledgments

mounted to canvas, 9 1/2 by 7 1/2 inches. Pierpont Morgan Library, New York. Bequest of John S. Thacher, 1985.46. The Pierpont Morgan Library/Art Resource, NY; 85, © Randy Wells/Getty Images; 86, Photo by Claire Garoutte, © Chihuly Studio; 87, © Kevin R. Morris/Corbis; 90, © Dran Hamilton and Tani Guthrie; 91, © Tony Freeman/PhotoEdit; 91, © Ariel Skelley/Corbis; 95, © Keith Carter/Photographer, Inc.; 98, Private Collection/Bridgeman Art Library; 100, Photo by Marcia Ward, courtesy of Glenna Goodacre Ltd.; 101, © Bob Krist/Corbis; 101, © Randy Wells/Corbis; 104, © Eric Meola/ImageBank/Getty Images; 105, © Dave Bartruff/Corbis; 105, © Michael Newman/PhotoEdit; 108, © Art Resource, NY. © 2004 Estate of Alexander Calder/Artists Rights Society (ARS), New York; 109, Photo by Jerry Anthony, courtesy of Stoner/Hatton Mobiles; 112, © Hillary Dragon/Dragon Clay Studio; 116, © George Disario/Corbis; 116, © Musée National d'Art Moderne, Centre Georges Pompidou, Paris/SuperStock; 116, © Robert Ginn/PhotoEdit; 118, © Francis G. Mayer/Corbis; 119(l), Auguste Renoir. Portrait of the Artist, 1897. Oil on canvas, 19 by 14 cm. Musée d'Orsay, Paris, France. © Réunion des Musées Nationaux/Art Resource, NY; 119(cl), © Getty Images; 119(cr), © Weinberg/Clark/Getty Images; 120, Digital image © The Museum of Modern Art/Licensed by Scala/Art Resource, NY; 121, Private Collection/Bridgeman Art Library. © 2004 Charly Herscovici, Brussels/Artists Rights Society (ARS), New York; 124, The Art Institute of Chicago. Mr. and Mrs. Frank G. Logan Prize Fund. Photograph © The Art Institute of Chicago. All Rights Reserved. 1935.313; 125, Musée d'Orsay, Paris/Lauros-Giraudon, Paris/SuperStock; 128, © Gerald French/Corbis; 129, © Joe McDonald/Corbis; 132, © SuperStock; 133, © National Museum of American Art, Washington, D.C./Art Resource, New York; 134, Virginia Museum of Fine Arts, Richmond. The Adolph D. and Wilkins C. Williams Fund. Photo by Katherine Wetzel/© Virginia Museum of Fine Arts; 138, © Gianni Dagli Orti/Corbis; 142, © Richard A. Cooke/Corbis; 143,© Trans-World Photos/SuperStock; 150, © Corbis; 150(cl), © James Urbach/SuperStock; 151, © Fiduciario en el Fideicomiso relativo a los Museos Diego Rivera y Frida Kahlo. Reproduction authorized by the Bank of Mexico, Mexico City; 152, Nam June Paik. Piano Piece, 1993. Albright-Knox Art Gallery, Buffalo, New York. Sarah Norton Goodyear Fund; 153(bl), © Christopher Felver/Corbis-Bettmann; 153, © Davies+Starr/Getty Images; 153, © Hans Neleman/Getty Images; 154, Courtesy of the Witte Museum, San Antonio, Texas; 158(t), 158(b), Monsters Inc., Mike Wazowski and James P. Sullivan (2001), Pixar/Walt Disney Co., courtesy of the Everett Collection; 159(cr), © Daniel Pangbourne Media/Getty Images; 162, © Corbis; 167, © Smithsonian American Art Museum, Washington, D.C./Art Resource, NY; 168, © Swim Ink/Corbis; 169, © Peter Cade/Getty Images; 172, © Smithsonian American Art Museum, Washington, D.C./Art Resource, NY; 173, Gift of Wallace and Wilhelmina Holladay/National Museum of Women in the Arts; 176, © SEF/Art Resource, NY; 181, © Daniel Bosler/Getty Images; 184, © Lake County Museum/Corbis; 184, © Daniel Pangbourne Media/Getty Images; 184, © Francis G. Mayer/Corbis; 184, © Daniel Pangbourne Media/Getty Images; 185, © SuperStock. © 2004 Estate of Alexander Calder/Artists Rights Society (ARS), New York; 186, Courtesy Bernice Steinbaum Gallery, Miami, FL; 187, Photo by Scott Nixon, © 1991. Photo courtesy of Bernice Steinbaum Gallery, Miami; 188, Morton Beebe, S.F./Corbis; 189, © The Newark Museum/Art Resource, NY; 192, © The Newark Museum/Art Resource, NY; 193, © Erich Lessing/Art Resource, NY; 200, © 2004 Red Grooms/Artists Rights Society (ARS), New York; 201, Courtesy Bernice Steinbaum Gallery, Miami, FL; 202, © Kevin Schafer/Corbis; 210, The Ogden Museum of Southern Art, University of New Orleans. Gift of the Roger H. Ogden Collection. © 1984 The Ida and Hugh Kohlmeyer Foundation; 211, © Stephen Marks/Getty Images; 211, © Getty Images; 214, © Jacqui Hurst/Corbis; 218, © Macduff Everton/Corbis; 218, © Henry Horenstein/Index Stock Imagery.

Back Matter

Page 220, © Getty Images; 220, © Getty Images; 220, © Corbis; 220, © Getty Images; 220, © Getty Images; 221, © Getty Images; 221, © digitalvisiononline.com; 222, © Darrell Gulin/Corbis; 222, © Eric Crichton/Corbis; 223, © Paul Chauncey/Corbis; 223(bl) © Corbis 223, © Corbis; 223, © Pat Doyle/Corbis; 224, © Robert Yin/Corbis; 224, © David Frazier/Corbis; 224, © Peter Dazeley/Corbis; 224, © Richard Hamilton Smith/Corbis; 224, © Charles Gold/Corbis; 224, © Lance Nelson/Corbis; 225, © The Purcell Team/Corbis; 225, © Lindsey P. Martin/Corbis; 225, © Nik Wheeler/Corbis; 226, © Corbis; 227, © Randy Faris/Corbis; 228, © Bob Krist/Corbis; 229, © Charles & Josette Lenars/Corbis; 230, © Mark Gibson/Corbis; 231, © Tom Bean/Corbis; 232, © Corbis; 233, © Getty Images; 238 (tl) © Burstein Collection/Corbis; 238 (bl) © David Young-Wolff/Photo Edit; 238 (tr) © Alan Schein Photography/Corbis; 239 (tl) © Dave Bartruff/Corbis; 239 (cl) © Getty Images; 239 (br) © Schafer/Smith/SuperStock; 240 (c) © Corbis; 240 (br) © Hubert Stadler/Corbis; 242 (tl), ©Francesco Venturi; Kea Publishing Service/Corbis; 242 (bl) © Danny Lehman/Corbis; 242 (cr) © Chris Rogers/Corbis; 243 (tl) © David Robinson/Corbis; 243 (bl) © Lindsay Hebberd/Cobis; 243 (tr) © Peter Barrett/Corbis; 243 (br) © Wolfgang Kaehler/Corbis; 244 (tl) © Gianni Dagli Orti/Corbis; 244 (cl) © Peter Cade/Getty Images; 244 (bl) © Bettmann/Corbis; 244 (br) © SW Productions/Getty Images; 245 (tl) © Michael Newman/Photo Edit; 245 (cl) © Geoffrey Clements/Corbis; 245 (bl) © Alan Schein/Corbis; 246 (tr) © Getty Images; 246 (cr) © Richard T. Nowitz/Corbis; 246 (br) © Corbis; 247 (tl), © David Young-Wolff/PhotoEdit; 247 (bl) © Harper-Collins Childrens Publishers; 247 (br) © Ryan McVay/Getty Images; 248 (bl) © Keren Su/Corbis